HIS
WRD
IS NOW

HIS
WORD
IS NOW

E. W. KENYON &
DON GOSSETT

WHITAKER
HOUSE

His Word Is Now

www.dongossett.com

ISBN: 978-1-62911-624-2
eBook ISBN: 978-1-62911-625-9
Printed in the United States of America
© 2016 by Debra Gossett

Whitaker House
1030 Hunt Valley Circle
New Kensington, PA 15068
www.whitakerhouse.com

Library of Congress Cataloging-in-Publication Data

Names: Gossett, Don, 1929-2014, author. | Kenyon, Essek William, 1867-1948, author.
Title: His word is now / by Don Gossett and E. W. Kenyon.
Description: New Kensington, PA : Whitaker House, 2016.
Identifiers: LCCN 2016000550 | ISBN 9781629116242 (trade pbk. : alk. paper)
Subjects: LCSH: Redemption—Christianity—Meditations. | Healing—Religious aspects—Christianity—Meditations. | Spiritual healing—Meditations.
Classification: LCC BT775 .G64 2016 | DDC 248.4—dc23
LC record available at http://lccn.loc.gov/2016000550

1 2 3 4 5 6 7 8 9 10 11 ⨀ 23 22 21 20 19 18 17 16

CONTENTS

PART I:

REDEMPTION IS NOW

1

THE JESUS NOW

E. W. KENYON

"Jesus Christ the same yesterday, and to day, and for ever."
—Hebrews 13:8

The word *Jehovah* has three tenses—past, present, and future. Likewise, there are three tenses in redemption: what God has done, what He is doing, and what He will do. What He was, He is. What He is now, He will be tomorrow.

The most unique feature of this is that the Word that He spoke back yonder is now. So you can see His Word is now. It is living now. It is authoritative now. It has power to save now. It has power to heal now.

Exodus 16:14–20 is the story of the giving of the manna. The manna had to be gathered every morning, and if any was left over the next day, it became sour, unfit to eat.

And so it is with the Word. It must be studied daily, meditated on daily, and fed on daily, or else it will lose its power.

The Israelites could not can the manna. They could not preserve it. They could not dry it. It was good for a day only. How striking is that thought.

Your experiences in Christ are like that. The experiences of yesterday are of no value now. Many of us have tried to preserve our experiences. It can't be done.

Furthermore, Jesus is the "now" Jesus. He is working now; He is now. When He said, *"Whatsoever ye shall ask of the Father in my name, he [shall] give it you"* (John 15:16), it was to last until He came back again.

When He said, *"In my name...they shall lay hands on the sick, and they shall recover"* (Mark 16:17–18), *that was to last until He came.*

The Word is as fresh as if it had been spoken yesterday.

When He said, *"If two of you shall agree on earth as touching any thing that they shall ask, it shall be done"* (Matthew 18:19), that is just as new and fresh as if it had been uttered this morning.

"If ye abide in me, and my words abide in you, ye shall ask what ye will, and it shall be done unto you" (John 15:7) is just as fresh as if Jesus had said it an hour ago.

No Word from God ever grows old. It has perennial freshness. It renews itself continually.

2

BEYOND THE END
OF OUR NOSE

DON GOSSETT

If we are to be true to Jesus' Great Commission, we must allow the Holy Spirit to give us a vision beyond the end of our nose. By that, I mean that it is not enough to be satisfied with ministering only in "Jerusalem." If we do not resist, grieve, or quench the Holy Spirit, surely we will receive His vision for the unreached in other nations of the world.

In my first years in the Lord's work, I focused my attention solely on ministry in Canada and the United States. What an undeniable stirring in my heart there was when the Holy Spirit revealed my responsibility to other countries.

Following the Lord's direction, we placed our daily radio program, *Bold Bible Living*, on Trans World Radio and began broadcasting the gospel in eighty-nine nations. Soon, we were receiving invitations to conduct crusades.

I vividly remember the thrill and challenge my wife and I sensed as we boarded an Air Canada jumbo jet in Vancouver to our first overseas crusades on an island in the West Indian Ocean. I was pumped high with excitement, and expected to be mightily used by God.

As we disembarked the plane, we were greeted with the initial blasts of heat and humidity. Little could we have anticipated the fierce testings we would experience in the days ahead.

Immediately, my physical body began reacting violently. I started hemorrhaging, which was accompanied by raging fevers and bone-shaking chills. For several days, I lingered between delirium and consciousness. The national pastors agreed to postpone our first crusade.

One hot afternoon, Joyce heard a sharp knock on the hotel room door. She quickly opened the door, and in walked the hotel manager, who peered through the mosquito net and saw me lying on the bed in a pool of perspiration and blood. She abruptly demanded that my wife remove me from the hotel, stating emphatically, "I don't want this man to die in my hotel!"

Sadly, we were required to book our flights back to Vancouver. I didn't understand why we had met with such adversities and dismal failure. A deep sense of defeat overwhelmed me. I had not even preached a single sermon or led one soul to Christ.

As the Air Canada jet descended into Vancouver, I turned to my wife, took her hand in mine, and pledged never to take her overseas again. Dejectedly, I said, "Honey, we tried our best, but it didn't work out. We will never leave the shores of North America again...."

I was so humiliated that I didn't even notify our children or church family that we were returning home. Instead, Joyce and I rented a car at the airport and drove home. After six weeks of physical battles, the hemorrhaging finally stopped. Soon, we settled back into life with our family and church.

But the vision for the lost in other countries still burned in our spirits. Within a year, our hearts were aflame with the fire and zeal for missionary evangelism.

Though I had said to my wife that we would never leave North America again, we did go overseas—scores and scores of times. God has greatly blessed us; countless thousands of precious people have received our ministry as we have proclaimed Christ in fifty-five nations.

If God has burdened your heart for the nations of the world, to see the redemption of the Lord reach the ends of the earth, I offer these suggestions to you:

1. Get God's direction. Pray that eight-word prayer made famous by Saul of Tarsus in Acts 9:6: *"Lord, what wilt thou have me to do?"* If your heart is yielded, the Holy Spirit will give you guidance.

2. Get provision for the vision. My dear friend, C. M. Ward, once said, "Next to salvation, money is your best friend." Traveling overseas and financing effective crusades for God's glory usually requires thousands of dollars; but where God guides, He provides!

3. Be bold and fearless! More than forty years ago when I worked with T. L. Osborn, he generously imparted to me many wonderful principles about taking the gospel around the world. I'll never forget one of his handwritten memos with this two-word admonition: "Be fearless!" That's just as good advice now as it was back in the 1960s. Be bold in your ministry among those who are bound by sin, sickness, demons, and fear.

4. Expect great things from God, attempt great things for God. This was the life motto of premier missionary William Carey. As we receive great things from God by His Word and Spirit, then we can attempt great things for God.

In the spring of 1979, I was a guest on Dr. Lester Sumrall's television program. While being interviewed by brother Sumrall, the Lord challenged me to win one million souls to Christ before my ministry concluded here on this earth. When I shared this vision with family and friends, nobody encouraged me. Some criticized me for such an encounter with God.

One million souls seemed totally impossible. Yet I knew the Lord had spoken to me. To personally encourage my own heart, I wrote these words in my daily journal: "I would rather attempt something great and fail than to attempt nothing and succeed. With Your help, Father, I will do my best!"

In late 1979, the Lord opened the doors of India to me. Crusading in India for much of the next twenty-three years was God's plan in fulfilling that vision of winning millions of souls.

If you receive and accept your part in God's plan for world evangelism, the Lord will lift your gaze beyond the end of your nose. Then you will help answer Jesus' striking prayer for laborers recorded in all four Gospels:

Say not ye, There are yet four months, and then cometh harvest? Behold, I say unto you, Lift up your eyes, and look on the fields; for they are white already to harvest.   (John 4:35)

3

SOME THINGS WE KNOW

E. W. KENYON

Paul's personal testimony thrills me. He said, *"For I know whom I have believed, and am persuaded that he is able to keep that which I have committed unto him against that day"* (2 Timothy 1:12).

You see, that puts the sense of mastery into a man's spirit, where reason can't travel, because the way is dark. The spirit has an inward light, and that inward light is shining upon the Word that cannot fail him.

You remember what Jesus said: *"If a man love me, he will keep my words: and my Father will love him, and we will come unto him, and make our abode with him"* (John 14:23).

That doesn't mean that He lives in the house only; He also lives in the heart. The Father and Jesus both are my Backers, my Providers, my Givers.

Why, Jesus is made unto me wisdom from God. (See 1 Corinthians 1:30.) I have more wisdom than any enemy. I have more ability. That came to me when I received His nature and life into my spirit. I am letting that nature dominate me.

I have love that makes me a master, a conqueror. His own love nature has lifted me out of bitter jealousy and selfishness. He has given to us a new self, Himself; a new nature, His nature; and new abilities, His abilities. They have swallowed us up. They dominate us in Christ.

You see, men, a man's spirit is shipped off first, then his reason faculties are filled with fear. It is just like an army that has lost its officers—panic seizes them.

Now, when that inward man, the inner spirit, is in union with God, the reasoning faculties may lose their poise and be filled with panic, but the spirit is still master. Though we are filled with outward fear, there is an inward courage that drives us on to win. Many boys have said to me, "Yes, I was frightened, I was filled with fear, and yet a sense of victory was in my spirit, and that was true."

So *"in all these things we are more than conquerors"* (Romans 8:37). We may see men defeated and fail around us, but we can't be conquered.

Say it over and over again, "I cannot be conquered because God is in me, and no one can conquer God."

4

GOD'S REVELATION TO THE APOSTLE PAUL

E. W. KENYON

In God's revelation of Jesus Christ to the apostle Paul, we see the supernatural element of Christianity in a light that the modern church has never seen.

Paul's revelation began with Jesus being made sin. It dealt with both what Jesus did and what was done to Him during the three days and three nights He was dead, until, finally, He arose from the dead, carried His blood into the heavenly Holy of Holies, and sat down at the right hand of the Father. That period covered the forty days from His crucifixion to His seating at the right hand of the Majesty on high.

It deals with three major facts: the great substitution of Christ, our being made new creations through the Holy Spirit, the Word, and what Jesus is doing for us now at the right hand of the Father. Let us look at what Christ did for us.

WHAT CHRIST DID FOR US

It is deeply important that the reader fully grasps these basic facts. Christ did not raise from the dead until He had broken Satan's dominion. It was imperative that Satan's authority be broken over man.

> *Who hath delivered us from the power of darkness, and hath*
> *translated us into the kingdom of his dear Son: in whom we*
> *have redemption through his blood, even the forgiveness of*
> *sins.*   (Colossians 1:13–14)

God delivered us out of Satan's authority. The word translated *"power"* here means "authority." God delivered us from the authority of darkness.

Then He translated us into the kingdom of the Son of His love. That is the new birth. That is recreation. We have our redemption. Every believer has been delivered out of Satan's authority and has been translated into the family of God. He is redeemed through Christ, and Satan has no more dominion over him.

> *For sin shall not lord it over you.*   (Romans 6:14, CTNT)

Sin is Satan. Satan shall not lord it over you. He has no more dominion over the believer than Pharaoh had over the children of Israel after they had crossed the Red Sea.

Satan has no dominion over you. He cannot put diseases upon you without your consent. It may be a consent of ignorance, but it is a consent.

Satan is defeated, conquered, as far as you are concerned. He is not only conquered, but God has made you a new creation over whom Satan has no dominion whatsoever.

> *Wherefore if any man is in Christ, he is a new creature: the*
> *old things are passed away; behold, they are become new. But*
> *all things are of God, who reconciled us to himself through*

Christ, and gave unto us the ministry of reconciliation.
(2 Corinthians 5:17–18 ASV)

The *"old things"* that have passed away are defeat, failure, weakness, poverty, sin, and spiritual death. We are new creations, and Jesus is the Lord of us. He has taken Satan's place, so he no longer has dominion over you. You need have no fear of him, for he has been conquered.

The Spirit, through the apostle Paul, gives us the position of the church. He said,

Nay, in all these things we are more than conquerors.
(Romans 8:37 ASV)

We have a complete and perfect redemption. This new creation has not only been declared righteous and made righteous, but both God and Jesus have declared him righteous.

Righteousness means the ability to stand in the Father's presence without a sense of guilt and with the same freedom and liberty that Jesus has.

The Revised Version marginal reading for Romans 3:26 declares, "That he might himself be righteous, and the righteousness of him that hath faith in Jesus." God has become your righteousness in Christ Jesus. Scripture says that God has made Jesus to be righteousness unto you. (See 1 Corinthians 1:30.) This is a most amazing fact. He does not stop there. Paul said, *"Him who knew no sin he made to be sin on our behalf; that we might become the righteousness of God in him"* (2 Corinthians 5:21 ASV).

If language means anything, then every believer stands complete in Christ:

And in him ye are made full [complete], who is the head of all principality and power.
(Colossians 2:10 ASV)

Of his fulness [or completeness] *we all received, and grace for grace.*   (John 1:16 ASV)

The believer is not a cringing suppliant, begging for favors. He is a son of God, an heir of God, a prince of God. He stands in the Father's presence unabashed and unafraid, because he has been made righteous with God's own righteousness, made free with God's own freedom. The Son has made you free. (See John 8:36.) You are free in reality. Disease and sickness have no dominion over you.

Had I the space, I could show you that you are not only redeemed as a new creation and the righteousness of God but you are a son of God, a member of His family. More than that, the Spirit who raised Jesus from the dead actually makes His home in your body.

You may never have given Him His place, or you may never have been conscious that God made His home in you or that you had the ability of God in you. You may have never taken advantage of the fact that your mind has been renewed and now you can know the will of God in reality.

Not only do you have God in you, but you have the name of Jesus and the authority of that name. In that name, if pain comes, you can lay hands on yourself and receive your deliverance. In that name, you can break the power of the adversary over your finances, your home, and your loved ones' bodies.

Limitless power and authority are given to every individual member of the body of Christ.

SOME OF THE HINDRANCES TO TRUE FAITH

Perhaps the most subtle and dangerous weapons of the devil are the sense of unworthiness and lack of faith. Your worthiness is Jesus Christ, the Righteous. You are the righteousness of God in Him. The sense of unworthiness is a denial of the substitutionary sacrifice of Christ and your standing in Christ, of Christ's right-eousness before the Father, which has been granted to you.

The second hindrance is that you have accepted hope and mental assent instead of faith. You never hope for a thing that you possess; you hope for the unpossessed. When you hope for your healing, for instance, it means that you have no faith for it; you expect to get it sometime. Hope is a beautiful delusion, and mental assent is a kindred of hope. Mental assent is a substitute for faith that the adversary has given to the church today.

Many declare that the whole Bible, from Genesis to Revelation, is true, but they do not accept miracles except in isolated cases. They assent to the truth of the Word, but they do not believe it. They say, "Yes, I believe the Bible is true," but never act on it. Believing is acting on the Word of God. There is no faith without action.

In the Weymouth translation of the Bible, James says that faith must have corresponding actions. "Faith without correspond-ing actions is dead." (See James 2:14.)

There can be no faith without action on the Word. I can assent to it, but I will remain as I am. I can admire it, but it is not mine.

The thing that the Scripture declares belongs to me. As soon as I found out the difference between mental assent and faith, I became a blessing to multitudes. Many have been healed over the radio when they stopped mentally assenting and acted on the Word.

Another enemy of faith is sense knowledge evidence. A man believes what he sees. He is like Thomas, who said, "I will not believe unless I can put my hand into His side." (See John 20:25.)

Jesus suddenly appeared and said, *"Reach hither thy finger…and put it into my side: and be not faithless, but believing"* (John 20:27 asv).

Faith is giving substance to things you have hoped for. It is a conviction of the reality of things that are not seen. (See Hebrews 11:1.) Faith is changing hope into reality and acting in the face of contrary evidence. The senses declare, "It cannot be," but faith shouts above the turmoil, "It is!" Faith counts the thing done before God has acted. That compels God's action. God is a faith God.

> *The worlds have been framed by the word of God, so that what*
> *is seen hath not been made out of things which appear.*
>
> (Hebrews 11:3 asv)

All God did at the beginning was say, *"Let there be...,"* and there was. All that faith has to say is, "Let there be perfect quietness in this man's body and spirit," and disease must go. Faith says, "Let there be plenty where poverty has reigned. Let there be freedom where bondage has held sway." These things must come to pass.

5

THIS IS MY HOUR OF POWER

DON GOSSETT

"According to the power that worketh in us."
—Ephesians 3:20

Below are powerful declarations that will remind you of the power living in you. Declare them when you fear or worry, when you're confused, when you don't know the way to go. God lives in you always.

1. I have power "working in me," for I have God within me. *"For it is God which worketh in you both to will and to do of his good pleasure"* (Philippians 2:13). God is actually working inside me, this I know. *"God hath spoken once; twice have I heard this; that power belongeth unto God"* (Psalm 62:11).

2. I have power "working in me" in the wonderful name of Jesus. Jesus has deputized me to use the authority of His name. (See John 14:13–14.) The name of Jesus is the name above all names. (See Philippians 2:9.) In the power of His name, I minister healing to the sick, cast out demons, and exercise the authority of Christ

in doing His works. (See John 14:12; Mark 16:17; Acts 3:16.)

3. This is my hour of power to witness for Christ with effectiveness, for He has endued me with power for this purpose. (See Acts 1:8; Luke 24:49.) As a witness endued with power, I am forever done with anemic, deficient, impotent living. This Spirit-power working in me invigorates my body, refreshes my mind, sustains me in trial, and fortifies me with boldness in witnessing. (See Romans 8:11; Acts 4:31.)

4. I know that *"all power...in heaven and in earth"* (Matthew 28:18) has been given to my Lord. Now, by His Spirit He indwells me, so I declare boldly, *"Greater is he that is in [me], than he that is in the world"* (1 John 4:4). Through the greater One who empowers me, I rout the railing accusations of Satan. (See Revelation 12:10.) I reject condemnation (see Romans 8:1), I refuse fear (see 2 Timothy 1:7), and I overcome his harassing ways (see 1 Peter 5:9).

5. I have power "working in me" when I boldly confess the Word. The Word is the sword of the Spirit that defeats Satan. My confession of the Word creates powerful results: healing, strength, money, and blessings.

6. I have power "working in me" when I heartily praise the Lord. Praise is power released unto God that brings a mighty response from Him. By simply praising the Lord, supernatural things happen all the time: bodies healed, demons cast out, peace restored to troubled hearts. O the power of praise! God is restoring to my life this power right now; I shall praise Him! Hallelujah, praise the Lord!

7. This is my hour of power.

Now unto him that is able to do exceeding abundantly above all that we ask or think, according to the power that worketh in us, unto him be glory in the church by Christ Jesus throughout all ages, world without end. Amen.

(Ephesians 3:20–21)

6

UNDERNEATH ARE THE EVERLASTING ARMS

E. W. KENYON

I did not know that He was the Undergirder, and I did not know that He would get under my burden and carry my load.

I had been a Christian for years. I had been holding on and doing the best I could. I had been surrendering and consecrating and giving up and yielding all. But I had never learned to take all. I had never learned to enjoy my present inheritance in Him.

I thought that I was so weak and bad that I had to continually consecrate and surrender. I did not know that I was created in Christ Jesus for good works. I did not realize that I was a partaker of the divine nature, that I had the strength of God in me. I did not know that He had created the universe and made His home in my body, so I was trying to fight the thing out the best I could.

I used to say, "I am holding on. It is the hard fight—the adversary is pressing me." I did not realize that underneath were the

everlasting arms. I did not realize that Satan was whipped, conquered, and defeated by the One who undergirded me. I did not
know that my Father was greater than all. That precious wonderful truth was veiled to this heart of mine.

Now I saw it and wondered why I had been blind so long. I
wondered why I hadn't seen it all before. I had seen that I was
walking with Him and that He always stepped in front of me
when danger came. I had seen the enemies scatter and never lift a
spear or sword or javelin because the greater One had conquered
them and they knew it.

But I did not know it.

Now I am getting to know Him. I am getting to rest in His
rest; to live in His love, in His quietness; to lie in the embrace
of His strength. He is feeding me with the Bread of heaven, the
manna of the Mighty. He has encouraged me with the wine of His
own making, and I am glad!

7

WHAT I CONFESS, I POSSESS

DON GOSSETT

What you confess, you possess. Here is a list of biblical declarations to confess:

First, I confess Jesus as my Lord; I possess salvation. (See Romans 10:9–10.)

Second, I confess that by His stripes, I am healed; I possess healing. (See Isaiah 53:5.)

Third, I confess that the Son has made me free; I possess absolute freedom. (See John 8:36.)

Fourth, I confess that "the love of God is shed abroad in my heart by the Holy Spirit" (see Romans 5:5); I possess the ability to love everyone.

Fifth, I confess that *"the righteous are bold as a lion"* (Proverbs 28:1); I possess lionhearted boldness in spiritual warfare.

Sixth, I confess that God "will never leave nor forsake me" (see Hebrews 13:5–6); I possess the presence of God each step I take.

Seventh, I confess that I am *"redeemed of the LORD"* (Psalm 107:2); I possess redemption benefits every day.

Eighth, I confess that the anointing of the Holy One abides in me (see 1 John 2:27) and has yoke-destroying results (see Isaiah 10:27).

Ninth, I confess in the name of Jesus that I can *"cast out devils"* (Mark 16:17); I possess dynamic deliverances as a devil-master.

Tenth, I confess that when I *"lay [my] hands on the sick...they shall recover"* (Mark 16:18); I possess healing for the oppressed.

Eleventh, I confess that I am a branch on the living Vine (see John 15:5); I possess Vine-life wherever I go.

Twelfth, I confess that I am *"the righteousness of God in [Christ]"* (2 Corinthians 5:21); I possess the ability to stand freely in God's holy presence and in Satan's presence as a victor!

Thirteenth, I confess that I am *"the temple of the living God"* (2 Corinthians 6:16); I possess God dwelling in me and walking in me!

Fourteenth, I confess that *"my God shall supply all [my] need"* (Philippians 4:19); I possess the supply of every need.

8

"YOUR HEAVENLY FATHER"

E. W. KENYON

Y*our heavenly Father"* (Matthew 6:32)—how tenderly beautiful it is.

At one time, the God of the Jews was so far away and unapproachable, but it is not so today. He knows my needs, He understands them, and He will meet them.

In John 10:27–29, Jesus said,

*My sheep hear my voice, and I know them, and they follow me: And I give unto them eternal life; and they shall never perish, neither shall any man pluck them out of my hand. My Father, which gave them me, **is greater than all**; and no man is able to pluck them out of my Father's hand.*

"My Father…is greater than all"—how it lifts the soul. How we need this precious, wonderful fact. The Father loves us, knows us, and cares for us. He is greater than any problem that confronts us and any circumstance that imprisons us. He is greater than poverty and greater than our enemies. Our Father is greater than all.

Midlife's bitter tears, temptations, and fear—my Father is greater than all.

How my heart has feasted upon this fact. This morning, facing all the financial problems of our ministry, to know that my Father is greater than all brings comfort.

John 16:27 says, *"The Father himself loveth you."* If a woman loves a man, and he loves her, it makes them one. Love makes two people one. Likewise, God's love for me and my response to it make us one.

He loves me. He is going to see to it that I do not have needs that will embarrass me, and He will help me carry my loads.

My Father loves me and gave His Son up for me. His love is not love for a multitude but love for me individually. I do not have to be afraid of life with a Lover like Him. I know that He will enable me to make good, to put things over. He will enable me to make a success of life. He loves me—but that is not all.

John 14:23 is perhaps the greatest Scripture in relation to this teaching. *"If a man love me, he will keep my words: and my Father will love him, and we will come unto him, and make our abode with him."*

Actually, He will come and live with us. The Father will come and make His home with us. That solves every problem. Every bill will be paid. Poverty can never come, for our Father God lives within us. There will be strength for every day. There will be healing for every disease, for the Father is going to live in us and make His home in us.

9

THE GREAT COMMISSION

E. W. KENYON

This is of the most vital importance to every believer. When Jesus was bidding good-bye to the disciples, He said,

> *All authority hath been given unto me in heaven and on earth. Go ye therefore, and make disciples of all the nations, baptizing them into the name of the Father and of the Son and of the Holy Spirit: teaching them to observe all things whatsoever I commanded you: and lo, I am with you always, even unto the end of the world.* (Matthew 28:18–20 ASV)

All authority has been given unto Jesus in heaven and on earth.

He did not need authority—He'd always had it—so why was it given to Him now that He was leaving the earth? It was given to Him because He was the Head of the church, the Firstborn from among the dead. He was the Lord of the church, His body. He was to use this authority through the church and for the church.

However, if there is no way for the church to use it, then it is ability like our unused capital. We have, for instance, billions of dollars worth of gold buried in the ground by the government. Some folks think this is a mark of poor judgment, for it could be in circulation and bringing blessing to the people.

The church has done the same thing with the "all authority" God gave to Jesus—it has buried it in its theology and creeds. No one seems to have been able to reach it, and it is doing no one any good. The church does not know that before Jesus went away, He gave it the power of attorney to use His name. This power of attorney gives the believer access to that *"all authority."*

> *Whatsoever ye shall ask* [or demand] *in my name, that will I do, that the Father may be glorified in the Son. If ye shall ask any thing in my name, I will do it.*   (John 14:13–14)

This is not prayer. It is using the name of Jesus to draw on this *"all authority."* The book of Acts gives case after case of men who tapped into that "all authority," and they were blessed by it.

That *"all authority"* is still available to those who use the name of Jesus. It has never been withdrawn.

If one part of that Great Commission has been abrogated, then all of it has been set aside. If one miracle has been set aside, then all miracles have been set aside, and the name of Jesus has no authority. But we know that His name was given to us for miracle work. Jesus said,

> *In my name shall they cast out devils; they shall speak with new tongues; they shall take up serpents; and if they drink any deadly thing, it shall not hurt them; they shall lay hands on the sick, and they shall recover.*   (Mark 16:17–18)

The adversary brings every one of these curses upon the church of God and the unsaved world. Satan holds men in bondage, fills them with fear of poison, and robs them of their testimony so that they do not speak in new tongues of deliverance and victory. He robs Christians of the ability to lay hands on the sick and see their loved ones recover. How? Sense knowledge gains mastery over the ministry.

Jesus said that as soon as men believe on Him, at once these signs accompany them. At once they begin to cast out demons. At once they begin to speak with tongues of power. At once they master disease. Serpents are typical of disease and demons.

> *So then the Lord Jesus, after he had spoken unto them, was received up into heaven, and sat down at the right hand of God. And they went forth, and preached everywhere, the Lord working with them, and confirming the word by the signs that followed.*   (Mark 16:19–20 ASV)

The Word that He had spoken, and the Word they dared to confess, was confirmed by signs that followed.

God's attitude toward sin and disease has never changed. Hebrews 13:8 declares that Jesus Christ is the same yesterday, today, and forever. He was opposed to disease then, and He is opposed to disease now. He suffered on account of sin, and His attitude toward sin is now how it was then.

So take the *"all authority"* that has been given to you and make disciples of all nations, fulfilling the Great Commission.

10

SALVATION IS IN THE SEATED CHRIST

DON GOSSETT

There is no salvation in the cross. Salvation is in the seated Christ and the empty tomb.

There are many Christians who will think that I have robbed them of their salvation when I tell them the truth about the cross, but it is nonetheless true.

Some churches have no seated Christ, no Savior at God's right hand. They simply have put a dead Christ on the cross. And the people today who tell you that they are living the "cross life" and that they are clinging to the cross and trusting in the cross have no resurrected Christ.

I wonder if you know that it is just as bad to sing a lie as it is to preach it. Think of the lyrics "Jesus, keep me near the cross, there a precious fountain."[1] He carried His blood into the Holy of Holies and procured for us an eternal redemption. I don't want to be kept

---

1. Fanny Jane Crosby, "Jesus, Keep Me Near the Cross," 1869.

near the cross. Why? Because we are *in* Christ. We have the life and nature of the Father in us.

Jesus said, *"I am the vine, ye are the branches"* (John 15:5). The Vine isn't on the cross. The Vine is in heaven. And it is *"Christ in you, the hope of glory"* (Colossians 1:27).

Do you know why some preach the cross and talk about the cross? Because they live in the "sense" realm. The cross is something they can see and feel. They can take hold of the little gold cross hanging on a chain around their necks, or pinned on the lapel of their coats, and feel very near to it. But Christ is not on the gold cross; Christ is seated at the right hand of the Father. He has put sin away. He has conquered Satan. He has risen from the dead. And, during the forty days He went and preached to the souls in paradise that had been covered by the blood of bulls and goats, He carried them the message of eternal life. He emptied paradise and took them all to heaven. They are there now.

When He carried His blood into heaven and the supreme court of the universe accepted it, it was poured out on the mercy seat in the presence of the Father, and He sat down; and He is still there today. His work was finished.

So His work began on the cross and ended on the throne. I can't understand why Christians make more of the cross than they do of the seated Christ and of their being seated together with Him.

The cross is where my Lord once hung, where God put our iniquity on Him, where God made Him to be sin for us, where God forsook Him, where God turned Him over to Satan, where sin triumphed, and where God ignored His prayer. No angels ministered to Christ there. Darkness cast a veil over the cross. It was where Love went the limit. He left His body hanging on the cross. He went to the place where we should have gone, and suffered in our stead until every claim was met. Then He was justified in Spirit, made alive in Spirit, and conquered Satan in Spirit as our Substitute. Then He entered into His own body, filled with immortality, and arose from the dead.

The seated Christ is a receipt in full for your healing. The seated Christ proves that He finished His work.

Always think of Satan as the defeated one, the one over whom you have dominion in Jesus' name. In that name, the new creation is the master of demons and disease and every circumstance that would hold you in bondage. We have a perfect redemption, a perfect new creation, and perfect union with Christ.

"*I am the vine, ye are the branches*" (John 15:5), Jesus said.

We have a message that brings success, health, happiness, and victory to every man. Every man is a failure outside of Christ. We hold God's solution to the human problem. The living Word on your lips makes you a victor, makes disease and poverty your servants. The living Word on your lips brings God on the scene, and brings victory and joy and success to the defeated.

11

FEEDING ON THE WORD

E. W KENYON

Look at the first chapter of John, verses 1–4:

> In the beginning was the Word, and the Word was with God, and the Word was God. The same was in the beginning with God. All things were made by him; and without him was not any thing made that was made. In him was life; and the life was the light of men.

You will see that Jesus is the Word, the Logos, and that we are to actually feed upon Him. "He that eats my body" (see Matthew 26:26; Mark 14:22; Luke 22:19; 1 Corinthians 11:24) really means "He that eats My words, feeds on them, and measures his strength by them…." In Matthew 4:4, Jesus said, "*Man shall not live by bread alone, but by every word that proceedeth out of the mouth of God.*" Man's spiritual nature demands spiritual food.

You see, many Christians that are dying from lack of nutritious food. They are weak and sickly in their prayer life, their love life, and their faith life—all because they are undernourished.

Preaching is made up of the theories of men rather than the Word of God. And all Christians need fed by the Word of God. Job 23:12 says, *"I have esteemed ["treasured up" ASV] the words of his mouth more than my necessary food."* This should be the continual attitude of the child of God toward the Bible: the Word of God having the first place in your daily reading and the first place in your daily meditation.

Acts 20:32 says, *"And now, brethren, I commend you to God, and to the word of his grace, which is able to build you up, and to give you an inheritance among all them which are sanctified."* It is the Word that gives us an inheritance in Christ.

> *But as it is in truth, the word of God, which also effectually worketh also in you that believe.*   (1 Thessalonians 2:13)

> *Let the word of Christ dwell in you richly.* (Colossians 3:16)

> *If ye abide in me, and my words abide in you, ye shall ask what ye will, and it shall be done unto you.*   (John 15:7)

It is the living, abiding Word in us that makes us effectual workers for Christ.

12

CONFESSION UNTO SALVATION

DON GOSSETT

Just as salvation, or everlasting life, the greatest of all God's gifts, is brought into our lives by the confession of our mouths, even so, all the other gifts, graces, and provisions of our Lord are confessed into reality. Confession precedes possession! What you confess, you possess! I so dare to say right now that you possess exactly what you have confessed. This works for both good and bad, health and sickness, courage and discouragement, plenty and lack, strength and weakness—you possess exactly what you confess. What you say is what you get!

Of course, the word *salvation* is one of the big words of the Bible. It is all-inclusive. It includes the supply of every need for both body and soul. Everything is provided in salvation.

It is very important that you watch your confession. Words of confession are faith words that work wonders. So are words of praise. David said, *"His praise shall continually be in my mouth"* (Psalm 34:1). Many Christians mistakenly have the praise of the devil in their mouths instead of the praise of the Lord.

For instance, if you say, "The devil has been after me all day long," you are praising the devil. If you say, "I am discouraged," you are praising the wrong person. If you say, "I am overwhelmed by my financial problems," you are praising the adversary, who has caused your financial dilemma. If you say, "It's so hard to have faith in God," you are praising the devil, who is the author of doubt. If you say, "I have a fear this might be cancer," you are yielding praise to the devil, who is the author of sickness. If you say, "I am so defeated," you are praising the devil, who defeats your life. If you say, "I just have no liberty," you are praising the devil, who has brought you into bondage. If you say, "I just don't believe God has forgiven my sins," you are praising the devil, who is the accuser of the brethren, the author of foul condemnation.

But if you say, "I always triumph in Christ," you are indeed praising the Lord. Oh, beloved, let His praise be continually in your mouth. How can you talk about your sickness and praise the devil, who has afflicted you? How can you talk weakness and praise that evil one, who has reduced you to weakness? How can you talk lack and honor the one who would strike you with poverty? How can you talk about your sleeplessness, thereby praising the thief who steals God's gift of sleep from you?

You must order your words aright, for God says, *"Whoso offereth praise glorifieth me: and to him that ordereth his conversation aright will I shew the salvation of God"* (Psalm 50:23).

If you say, "I just can't love others," you are praising the author of hate, who would rob you of your rightful heritage of the love of God in your heart. If you say, "I just don't feel the presence of God with me anymore," you are praising the devil, who would void the sure Word of God, which declares, *"I will never leave thee, nor forsake thee"* (Hebrews 13:5). If you say, "I just have no anointing," you are praising the devil, who tries to make the Word of God— which emphatically declares, *"The anointing which ye have received of him abideth in you"* (1 John 2:27)—of no effect. If you say, "I just can't do anything against this demonical attack against me," you are praising the devil, who causes you to disbelieve the words of Jesus, who said, "*These signs shall follow them that believe; in my name shall they cast out devils*" (Mark 16:17).

You must not give praise to the devil, even though you've done it unknowingly or ignorantly. Your testimony must be, "*I will bless the* LORD *at all times: his praise shall continually be in my mouth*" (Psalm 34:1). What you say is what you get. Again, David said, "*O magnify the* LORD *with me, and let us exalt his name together*" (Psalm 34:3). By your words, you can either magnify the Lord or magnify the devil.

If you say, "I am free '*in the liberty wherewith Christ hath made* [me] *free*'" (Galatians 5:1), you magnify the Lord. If you say, "I am rejoicing because my name is written down in heaven" (see Luke 10:20), you magnify the Lord. If you say, "*God hath not given* [me] *the spirit of fear*" (2 Timothy 1:7), you magnify the Lord. If you say, "God '*hath blessed* [me] *with all spiritual blessings*'" (Ephesians 1:3), you magnify the Lord. If you say, "*Truly I am full of power by the spirit of the* LORD" (Micah 3:8), you magnify the Lord. If you say, "*The* LORD *is the strength of my life*" (Psalm 27:1), you magnify the Lord. If you say, "As my days are, so shall my strength be" (see Deuteronomy 33:25), you magnify the Lord.

However, if you say, "I can't win my loved ones to Christ," you magnify the devil. If you say, "I can't receive my healing," you magnify the devil. If you say, "I can't pay my bills," you magnify the devil. If you say, "I can't witness in power. I'm so weak and anemic as a Christian when it comes to giving my testimony," you magnify the devil. If you say, "I just can't get my prayers answered," you magnify the devil. If you say, "I can't overcome my overweight condition," you magnify the devil. If you tell people your troubles in order to get their sympathy, you magnify the devil.

Magnifying the Lord is a vital secret of active faith. Paul revealed to us a tremendous faith secret in Philemon 1:6: "*That the communication of thy faith may become effectual by the acknowledging of every good thing which is in you in Christ Jesus.*" Notice that your faith becomes effective when you acknowledge every good thing which is in you, even Christ Jesus.

The word *"acknowledging"* is another word for "confessing" or "affirming." Acknowledging the good things that are in you in Christ Jesus makes your faith effectual. Notice that it is the good things within you *"in Christ Jesus,"* not in your own attainments.

The more I deal with people and listen to their baffling statements of how hard it is to trust God, I'm convinced that this is one of the devil's subtle devices—of which we must not be ignorant—making us focus our attention on our past sins, failures, weaknesses, and mistakes. You must resist the devil, and he will flee from you. (See James 4:7.)

"Thy faith may become effectual by the acknowledging of every good thing which is in you in Christ Jesus." Your faith is set on fire by acknowledging every good thing in you in Christ Jesus. Acknowledge your possessions in Christ and then go to the level of confession. Of course, if you have a bad confession, a negative confession, acknowledging things other than the good things in you in Christ Jesus, you go to the level of defeat, failure, weakness and lack. Refuse to do that.

13

I WILL DELIVER THEE

E. W. KENYON

"Thou calledst in trouble, and I delivered thee."
—Psalm 81:7

This sounds like our own personal experience—a leaf out of our own history. We called, and He heard us!

In a meeting the other day, I asked for a show of hands of those who'd had their prayers answered since our meeting the previous week. Faces aglow, hands uplifted, and voices filled with praises told of answered prayers. Many called in their trouble, and God answered in faithfulness. We came with our burdens and heartaches, and He took them. We came with our cares, and He assumed them. We came with our diseases, and He healed them.

Our hearts are filled with praise and worship and adoration because we know that the God of the whole universe is our own very Father. He loves us. If He carried Israel in His bosom, He carries us upon His heart. If He engraved them upon the palm of His hand, He has hidden us away in Christ.

Oh, the wealth of the riches of His glory and love! We did call, and He has answered. *"Whatsoever ye shall ask in my name, that will I do*" (John 14:13), said the Master. Mark you, He said, "*Will I do.*"

You ask, you pray, and you intercede; and He will answer, He will do, and He will work.

14

THE HIGH PRIESTHOOD OF JESUS

E. W. KENYON

Jesus' ministry at the right hand of the Father is one of the rarest features of the Pauline revelation. The problem of the authorship of Hebrews is settled—Hebrews is a part of that revelation. No one else could have given it as Paul has given it to us. It is a revelation of what Jesus did from the time He had been made sin on the cross until He sat down on the right hand of the Father. That entire work is given to us in this wonderful unveiling.

Not only did Paul make known what Christ did for us in His substitution, but he has made known what the Holy Spirit, through the Word, on the ground of the substitutionary work of Christ, does in the individual life.

There are really four phases of this revelation. First, what Christ did for us. Second, what the Holy Spirit, through the Word, does in us. Third, what Jesus is doing now for us at the right hand of the Father. Fourth, what His love does through us in ministry.

We spend much time studying what Christ has done for us but very little time on what He does in us, and even less on what He is now doing in His great, high priestly office at the right hand of the Father.

His entire ministry for us would have been a total failure had He not carried it on till now at the right hand of the Father.

Jesus died as the Lamb. He arose as the High Priest. His first ministry, after He arose from the dead, is illustrated in John 20:15–18, which records Jesus' meeting with Mary after His resurrection. She fell down at His feet, and no wonder. He said to her, *"Touch me not; for I am not yet ascended to my Father: but go to my brethren, and say to them, I ascend unto my Father, and your Father; and to my God, and your God."*

What did He mean? He died as the substitute Lamb. He arose as the High Priest.

> *Wherefore it behooved him in all things to be made like unto his brethren, that he might become a merciful and faithful high priest in things pertaining to God, to make propitiation for the sins of the people.*   (Hebrews 2:17 ASV)

He is a merciful and faithful High Priest, not in things pertaining to man but in things pertaining to God. The claims of justice had to be satisfied and the needs of man had to be met. It was necessary that as a High Priest, Jesus should make propitiation for the sins of the people. This is recorded in Hebrews 9:11–12 (ASV):

> *But Christ having come a high priest of the good things to come, through the greater and more perfect tabernacle, not made with hands, that is to say, not of this creation, nor yet through the blood of goats and calves, but through his own blood, entered in once for all into the holy place, having obtained eternal redemption.*

"Christ having come"—from whence did He come? Out of the place where He had gone as a substitute, when He had met the claims of justice; where He had satisfied the claims of the supreme court of the universe against rebellious humanity. He had to carry His blood into the heavenly Holy of Holies and seal the document of our redemption with it. Now His blood is the guarantor of the integrity of our redemption.

Just as the high priest under the first covenant carried the blood into the Holy of Holies once a year and made a yearly atonement, Jesus carried His own blood in and made an eternal redemption once for all. To the Israelites, atonement simply meant to cover the sin, which were borne away by the scapegoat.

The sin nature in man that caused him to break the law (not the act itself, but the cause of the act) was antagonistic against God and had to be covered. To be clear, it was not the sins man had committed that needed to be put away; it was man's sin nature that had to be put away. That sin nature was spiritual death, the nature of Satan. Now Jesus came and put that nature away by the sacrifice of Himself.

> But now once at the end of the ages hath he been manifested to put away sin by the sacrifice of himself.
>
> (Hebrews 9:26 ASV)

Our sins were small things that could be wiped out. But our sin nature required God's own beloved Son to become sin, that we might become the righteousness of God in Him. He took our sin that we might become righteous. He took our spiritual death that we might have eternal life. He took our ostracism, our outlawed nature, that we might become sons of the Father.

Oh, the unmeasured grace of God unveiled in the sacrifice of Jesus! He carried His own blood into the heavenly Holy of Holies and, instead of making the yearly atonement, gave us an eternal redemption.

Wherefore it behooved him in all things to be made like unto his brethren, that he might become a merciful and faithful high priest in things pertaining to God.   (Hebrews 2:17 ASV)

He is a merciful and faithful High Priest. God had to be satisfied, the claims of justice had to be met. So He was made sin, was under condemnation, and for three *days* and three nights was locked up in hell, the prison house of death. The supreme court was able to absolutely justify Him as our substitute and declare Him utterly righteous. He met the demands of justice and was liberated.

God said of Him, *"This day have I begotten thee"* (Psalm 2:7 ASV).

What day was He begotten? The third day down in the prison house of death, when He was born again of the Spirit. That was His new birth, when we were recreated, *"for we are his workmanship, created in Christ Jesus"* (Ephesians 2:10).

He was justified in spirit there. Not only was He declared righteous, but He was made righteous with the very nature of God. Now having been made righteous, having conquered Satan, stripping him of his authority, He arose from the dead, and the supreme court of the universe absolutely puts the stamp of approval on His work for us. Then He was able to go into the heavenly Holy of Holies and sit down at the right hand of the Majesty on high.

He has made propitiation for our sins. That word *propitiation* means "substitution," so He has made substitution for the sins of the people.

Having Himself suffered being tempted, He is able to succor those who are tempted.

Hebrews 3:1 (ASV) says, *"Wherefore, holy brethren, partakers of a heavenly calling, consider the Apostle and High Priest of our confession, even Jesus."*

Christianity is called a *"confession."* The finished work of Jesus Christ is called a *"confession."* Now you can understand Romans 10:9–10:

> *If thou shalt confess with thy mouth the Lord Jesus, and shalt believe in thine heart that God hath raised him from the dead, thou shalt be saved. For with the heart man believeth unto righteousness; and with the mouth confession is made unto salvation.*

Christianity is a confession. It is a confession of the finished work of Jesus. It is a confession that He is seated at the right hand of the Father, having perfectly redeemed us. It is a confession of our sonship, of our place in Christ, of our rights and privileges. It is a confession of our supremacy over disease and weakness, over Satan in the name of Jesus. What a confession that is!

Hebrews 4:14–16 (ASV) carries us a step further in the development of this high priestly ministry of Jesus.

> *Having then a great high priest, who hath passed through the heavens, Jesus the Son of God, let us hold fast our confession. For we have not a high priest that cannot be touched with the feeling of our infirmities; but one that hath been in all points tempted like as we are, yet without sin. Let us therefore draw near with boldness unto the throne of grace, that we may receive mercy, and may find grace to help us in time of need.*

The entire ministry of Jesus swings about this high priestly office. As a High Priest, He carried His blood into the Holy of Holies. As a High Priest, He sat down at the right hand of the Majesty on high. He is the mediatorial High Priest between God and man. No man can reach the Father but through Him. Jesus said, *"I am the way, the truth, and the life: no man cometh unto the Father, but by me"* (John 14:6). Peter said, *"And in none other is there salvation: for neither is there any other name under heaven, that is given among men, wherein we must be saved"* (Acts 4:12 ASV). Jesus is the only Way into the Father's presence without condemnation.

Is it any wonder that the early church was called *"the Way"?*

And asked of him letters to Damascus unto the synagogues, that if he found any that were of the Way, whether men or women, he might bring them bound to Jerusalem.

(Acts 9:2 ASV)

But when some were hardened and disobedient, speaking evil of the Way before the multitude, he departed from them, and separated the disciples, reasoning daily in the school of Tyrannus.   (Acts 19:9 ASV)

And about the time there arose no small stir concerning the Way.   (Acts 19:23 ASV; see also Acts 16:17; 24:14, 22; Isaiah 30:21; 35:8)

He is not only the Lord High Priest, the Mediator, but the moment a man accepts Christ, He becomes a high priestly Intercessor. He ever lives to make intercession for the believer. (See Isaiah 53:12; Romans 8:34; Hebrews 7:25.) What a ministry, what a service. He does not have a chance to take a vacation. He has no opportunity to step aside for a moment. No one else can act as high priest, mediator, and intercessor.

But He has another important ministry: He is the Advocate.

When the believer is tempted and Satan gains the mastery over him, he cries out in agony for mercy, and Christ whispers, *"If we confess our sins, he is faithful and righteous to forgive us our sins, and to cleanse us from all unrighteousness"* (1 John 1:9 ASV). Then He climaxes it by saying, *"My little children, these things write I unto you that ye may not sin. And if any man sin, we have an Advocate with the Father, Jesus Christ the righteous"* (1 John 2:1 ASV).

He is righteous, so He can go into the Father's presence when we lose the sense of righteousness by our wrongdoings. As our Advocate, He restores to us our lost sense of righteousness.

He is the Lord and Head of the church. David prophesied of Him in Psalm 23:1, "*The* Lord *is my shepherd; I shall not want.*"

He is the Caretaker, Lover, and Bridegroom of the body. He is the Firstborn from the dead, the Head of all principalities and powers. He is the risen Lord, seated at the Father's right hand.

Follow me through the entire epistle of Hebrews, and you will find a continual unveiling of these different phases of His high priestly ministry.

> Havingthenagreathighpriest,whohathpassedthroughtheheav-ens, Jesus the Son of God, let us hold fast our confession.
> (Hebrews 4:14 asv)

What is our confession? It is our redemption, our recreation, our union with the Father in Christ, our victory over circumstances and demons and diseases, and our independence of natural law in Christ.

This High Priest, knowing that man has received an inferiority complex on account of spiritual death, says,

> *For we have not a high priest that cannot be touched with the feeling of our infirmities; but one that hath been in all points tempted like as we are, yet without sin. Let us therefore draw near with boldness unto the throne of grace, that we may receive mercy, and may find grace to help us in time of need.*
> (Hebrews 4:15–16 asv)

The word "*boldness*" means "freedom of speech." In the Pishito (the oldest Syriac version of the New Testament), there is a marginal reference that reads "barefacedness." We are coming without any sense of guilt or sin, as a child would come to his earthly parent.

"*For every high priest, being taken from among men*" (Hebrews 5:1 ASV), has infirmities. Jesus had no infirmities. He had nothing but what He took on from us. He did not come from the seed of Levi. He was not in the priesthood by birth. He is a Priest after an order on the part of God.

(*The* LORD *sware and will not repent himself, Thou art a priest for ever*); *by so much also hath Jesus become the surety of a better covenant.* (Hebrews 7:21–22 ASV)

He is a High Priest, the surety of this new covenant, which heads up in Him. He was the sacrifice of the covenant. His blood was the blood of the covenant. His life was the life of the covenant. Now He is the surety of it.

Every Scripture from Matthew to Revelation is backed up by the Lord Jesus Himself. His very throne is back of every Word.

Just as God became the surety of the Abrahamic covenant, Jesus now is the surety of this new covenant. And He can be, because He abides forever. His priesthood is unchangeable.

Wherefore also he is able to save to the uttermost them that draw near unto God through him, seeing he ever liveth to make intercession for them. For such a high priest became us. (Hebrews 7:25–26 ASV)

"*For such a high priest became us*"—I think there is no sweeter expression in the entire revelation than this. Consider Him in all His grace and beauty and His overflowing love. It is such a High Priest who becomes us. We are new creations. We are in the beloved. We are the sweetest, most beautiful things that the Father has. We are members of His own body.

Christ says in verse 27 (ASV), "*First for his own sins, and then for the sins of the people: for this he did once for all, when he offered up himself.*" He was made sin for us. He made one sacrifice for sins forever, then He sat down at the right hand of the Majesty on high. (See

Hebrews 10:12.) Do you realize what it means when it says He sat down? It means that your redemption is a completed thing. You are healed. You are as well as Jesus, in the mind of the Father. You are an absolute overcomer. Poverty, want, and need are things of the past.

> *That we may receive mercy, and may find grace to help us in time of need.*   (Hebrews 4:16 ASV)

> *My God shall supply every need of yours.*
>   (Philippians 4:19 ASV)

> *Your heavenly Father knoweth that ye have need of all these things.*   (Matthew 6:32 ASV)

Jesus demonstrated this in His earth walk. He fed the multitudes. He gave the disciples that great draft of fish. He turned water into wine. He healed the sick and met every need of man. That is my Lord. He is the mediator of this new covenant. He stands between humanity and the Father with the pierced hands and the wounded side and the thorn-scarred brow.

He is the mediator. Do you think He will turn anyone away who comes to the Father? Never! Every unsaved man has a legal right to eternal life. Jesus takes his part and vouches for him the moment he says, "God, I will take your Son as my Savior and confess Him as my Lord."

Jesus' high priestly ministry meets every need of the believer from the moment he is born again until he is ushered into the presence of the Father at the end of life.

15

NO CORRUPT COMMUNICATION

DON GOSSETT

"Let no corrupt communication proceed out of your mouth, but that which is good to the use of edifying, that it may minister grace unto the hearers."
—Ephesians 4:29

This Scripture is a strong, direct command to every Christian. Corrupt communication out of your mouth not only means gossiping, griping, groaning, faultfinding, cursing, and other wrong uses of the tongue, but it means unedifying, unprofitable speech, which does not build up. Our words are to minister grace to the hearers. Our words should minister even to our own hearts as we hear them spoken. That's why we should say what God says about every detail of our lives.

Your speech is corrupt if you say, "I have to be sick every day." Isaiah 33:24 gives a biblical pattern for the right conversation of a child of God:

And the inhabitant shall not say, I am sick.

Your speech is corrupt if you say, "God is withholding something from me." Psalm 84:11 promises, *"No good thing will he withhold from* them that walk uprightly." Jesus said, "*If ye abide in me, and my words abide in you, ye shall ask what ye will, and it shall be done unto you*" (John 15:7). When God's Word abides in you, you will speak that Word. Again, Jesus taught, "*Out of the abundance of the heart the mouth speaketh*" (Matthew 12:34). What is in the heart will come forth through the mouth. That's why you must be nourished with God's Word and have it in your heart, so it comes to the forefront in every situation.

When it comes to words, you are commanded to "*speak as the oracles of God*" (1 Peter 4:11). If you speak as the oracles of God, you will say, "*The LORD...delivered me from all my fears*" (Psalm 34:4), "*The LORD...saved* [me] *out of all* [my] *troubles*" (Psalm 34:6), and "*The eyes of the LORD are upon the righteous, and his ears are open unto their cry*" (Psalm 34:15).

On the other hand, if you speak as the oracles of Satan, you will say, "God is so far away; He does not hear me." But if you speak as the oracles of God, you will say, "*The righteous cry, and the LORD heareth, and delivereth them out of all their troubles*" (Psalm 34:17).

If you speak as the oracles of Satan, you will say, "I pray for my family to be saved, but it doesn't do any good." But Jesus promised the Spirit-filled Christian that "*the Holy Ghost shall teach* [them] *in the same hour what* [they] *ought to say*" (Luke 12:12). When the Holy Spirit inspires your words, He will cause you to make confessions of the Word unto healing, happiness, and health instead of sickness, sin, and sorrow. When the Holy Spirit gives you words to speak, He will compel you to confess plenty, prosperity, and power instead of discouragement, despair, and disease. When the Holy Spirit has control of your words, He will enable you to say with authority, "*Such as I have give I thee: in the name of Jesus Christ of Nazareth rise up and walk*" (Acts 3:6).

Let the word of Christ dwell in you richly in all wisdom; teaching and admonishing one another in psalms and hymns and spiritual songs, singing with grace in your hearts to the Lord.

(Colossians 3:16)

If His Word dwells in your heart richly, you will encourage people and not discourage them. If His Word dwells in you richly, you will speak a word in due season:

> The Lord GOD hath given me the tongue of the learned, that I should know how to speak a word in season to him that is weary: he wakeneth morning by morning, he wakeneth mine ear to hear as the learned. (Isaiah 50:4)

When the Word dwells in you richly, you will speak that Word in face of all situations. Leo Harris of Australia said, "It is very hard and well nigh impossible for you to believe that God is for you if you continually talk about the things that are against you." Two more powerful statements are *"Death and life are in the power of the tongue"* (Proverbs 18:21) and *"With the increase of his lips shall he be filled"* (Proverbs 18:20).

Quoting Leo Harris again,

> So we see the tremendous power in the words that we speak. Our tongues determine life or death, healing or sickness, victory or defeat.
>
> Our words fill us the same as the food we eat. More people are sick because of the words they speak than because of what they eat! Someone said, "Stomach ulcers are not caused by what you eat but by what's eating you!"

What shall we say? What do you say? Do you say that God is for you? Do you declare the promises of God? Do your words agree with God's Word? The Bible abounds with promises for you—God's words for the blessing of your life. That's what God says, but what do you say? Why not start today to say what God says, to agree with God's Word, and to declare with your lips the mighty promises of God for you?

16

GOD IS A FAITH GOD

E. W. KENYON

I never knew the "why" of faith until I read Hebrews 11:3 (ASV):

By faith we understand that the worlds have been framed [or created] by the word of God, so that what is seen hath not been made out of things which appear.

Then, like a flash, I grasped the secret of Genesis 1:1: *"In the beginning God created...."* How did He create? By the word of faith. He said, *"Let there be..."* (Genesis 1:3). He created with words. Jesus knew the secret of words—He healed the sick with words, He raised the dead with words, He stilled the sea with words: *"Peace, be still"* (Mark 4:39).

Peter healed the sick by using the name of Jesus. Paul cast out demons by saying, "In the name of Jesus Christ, come out." (See Acts 16:18.)

They used words that were born of faith. They were faith words. We become the sons of God, partakers of His very nature, by acting with words. We become faith men and women when we use faith words and produce faith results.

"Faith in my faith"—the first time those words came to me, they startled me. I began to examine myself and ask, "Why is it that people haven't faith in their own faith?" They have faith in my faith. You see, I receive letters from people in many faraway countries asking for prayer. Why? Because they don't have confidence in their own faith. For some reason, they do not believe in themselves. They do not believe in what Christ has wrought for them, or who they are in Christ. They feel that they are not good enough, that their faith is not strong enough. They are acquainted with all their failings and weaknesses. They accept every condemnation from the pulpit. They are always willing to believe anything against themselves, such as their unworthiness, their unfitness, their weakness, and their lack of faith.

Here are some facts: The Father has no favorites. Every person born into His family has the same redemption. He has been redeemed out of the hand of his enemy, who was conquered for him personally. He can say, "'[Christ] *was delivered up for* [my] *trespasses, and was raised for* [my] *justification*'" (Romans 4:25 ASV). Furthermore, he can confidently say, "'[Christ] *delivered* [me] *out of the power of darkness, and translated* [me] *into the kingdom of the Son of his love; in whom* [I] *have* [my] *redemption, the forgiveness of* [my] *sins*'" (Colossians 1:13–14).

It is a personal, an absolute redemption from the dominion of the adversary. Christ was your substitute. When Jesus put Satan to naught and stripped him of his authority, it was you, in Christ, who did that work. Christ acted in your stead; He did it for you. You can say, "In Christ, I conquered Satan. I stripped him of his authority, and when Jesus arose from the dead, I arose with Him." (See Colossians 2:15.)

In addition, you can confidently say, "But God, being rich in mercy, for His great love wherewith he loved me, even when I was dead through my trespasses and sins, made me alive together with Christ (by grace have I been saved, or healed), raised me up with Him, and made me to sit with Him in the heavenly places, in Christ Jesus." (See Ephesians 2:4–6 ASV.)

It is when you take your place and begin to assume your rights and privileges that God responds to you. You have the same eternal life that Jesus had. *"He that hath the Son hath life"* (1 John 5:12). You have the Son; therefore, you have life.

Now, you may say, "I have taken Jesus Christ as my Savior. I have confessed Him as my Lord. God has given to me eternal life, His own nature. I am now a new creation, created in Christ Jesus, and I have God's ability to perform the good works that were afore prepared that I should walk in them.

"I have God's ability, because I have God's nature. I have the same great, mighty Spirit who raised Jesus from the dead dwelling in me. *'Greater is he that is in* [me], *than he that is in the world'* (1 John 4:4)."

Scripture says, *"Him who knew no sin* [God] *made to be sin on our behalf; that we might become the righteousness of God in him"* (2 Corinthians 5:21 ASV).

You can say, "I have become the righteousness of God in Him. There is therefore now no condemnation to me, because I am in Christ Jesus." (See Romans 8:1.)

That righteousness gives you the privilege of standing in the Father's presence as though you have never sinned. You have His nature. He is your Father, and you are His very own child. As a son or daughter, you have the legal right to use the name of Jesus. No one has a better right to use the name of Jesus than you and your brothers and sisters in Christ.

Now say with me,

Jesus declares that whatever I ask in His name, He will give it to me. Fearlessly, I take my place. I lay my hands upon my loved one who is sick and say, "In the name of Jesus, disease, leave this body; demon, leave this body and go off into the abyss where you belong. Don't you ever touch this loved one again."

Christ said to me that they who believe should lay hands on the sick, and they should recover. *"In my name shall they cast out demons"* (Mark 16:17 ASV). I accept this at face value, and I act upon it, because Christ said it to me.

17

THE LITTLE THINGS

DON GOSSETT

John declared, *"Never man spake like this man"* (John 7:46).

This is a message on little things—little but yet so vitally important. This is a message on words. Our life is made up of words—spoken words, written words, words set to music, and so forth.

What a blessing our words can be! Yet what a curse they can be to the man who does not realize their importance. In a most striking statement, Jesus said, *"By thy words thou shalt be justified, and by thy words thou shalt be condemned"* (Matthew 12:37).

Words can strengthen the weak, encourage the discouraged, lift up the fallen, sustain the weary, heal the sick, dominate circumstances, and minister grace to the hearer. However, words can also snare the soul, destroy faith, spiritually and mentally poison lives, tear down instead of build up, and deceive and defeat people. When we realize that nearly all heartache and misunderstanding come to us through words, we will realize the value of words.

You remember Job's comforters. They ought to be a living lesson to every one of us. Job cried, *"How long will you...crush me with words?"* (Job 19:2 NIV). That is what his comforters were doing. They came as comforters but stayed as condemners.

Our business is not to crush and hurt people with words.

The Lord God ["Jehovah" (ASV)] hath given me the tongue of the learned, that I should know how to speak a word in season to him that is weary: he wakeneth morning by morning, he wakeneth mine ear to hear as the learned. (Isaiah 50:4)

In the life and ministry of Jesus, we see the profound effect and power of words. At the very beginning of His ministry, His marvelous words stood out. When He went to Nazareth, He read Scripture from the book of Isaiah and announced His divine commission. The people *"all bare him witness, and wondered at the gracious words which proceeded out of his mouth"* (Luke 4:22). The people were astonished that He spoke not as the scribes and Pharisees but rather as a person who had authority.

Dr. Kenyon wrote these very helpful and profound words:

The believer who is always confessing his sins and his weaknesses is building weakness, failure, and sin into his consciousness. If we do sin, when we confess it, *"he is faithful and just to forgive us our sins, and to cleanse us from all unrighteousness"* (1 John 1:9). When that confession has been made, we never refer to it again. It is not just past history, because history can be remembered. It is as though it had never been. We should never remind ourselves or the Lord of our failings or of our past mistakes. They are not! If you confess anything, confess that you stand complete in Him—that what God has said in regard to your mistakes and blunders is absolutely true. We should never confess our sins to people. We may have to ask forgiveness of them, but then we are to forget them. Never tell anyone about your weakness or about your past blunders and failures. They will not forget them and sometime will remind you of them. If you tell it to anyone, tell it to the Lord and then forget it.[2]

---

2. Don Gossett and E. W. Kenyon, *The Power of Your Words* (New Kensington, PA: Whitaker House, 1977, 1981).

18

MY "NEVER AGAIN" LIST

DON GOSSETT

The Lord first thrust me into radio ministry when I was only twenty-one back in 1951. He reaffirmed that calling to radio ministry in 1961, when once again, I embarked on a daily radio ministry. Then in 1962, while ministering to our precious Indian friends at Fort Rupert, British Columbia, God decisively called me to a far-reaching radio ministry. At that point, I had been only a provincial radio broadcaster, but God had suddenly called me to become a national and international voice for Him by means of the radio. What a delight it has been to obey this sacred calling and to be used of God to share the gospel message with eighty-nine different countries.

In addition to this reaffirmed calling of the Lord to radio ministry, I had a great visitation from the Lord while conducting meetings in Longview, Washington. I was there for five weeks, ministering twice daily and meeting with God in personal fellowship for many sweet hours alone in my room.

There in Longview, the Holy Spirit lead me into a time of great study of the Word on the important topics of confession, the power of my words in relation to what I would receive from the Lord, overcoming negative confessions, and allowing the Word of God to prevail. The Lord spoke to my heart as a read these verses in Malachi:

> *Your words have been stout against me, saith the* Lord.
>
> (Malachi 3:13)

> *Ye have wearied the* Lord *with your words.* (Malachi 2:17)

I pondered how my words had been stout against the Lord and how I had wearied Him with my words. He spoke to me that my words had been out of harmony with His Word and that I had been speaking about my financial struggles and other negative factors more than I had confessed His conquering Word.

Again, He dealt with me with Scripture: *"Can two walk together, except they be agreed?"* (Amos 3:3). I realized that in order to walk with the Lord in the financial supply I was so lacking and in strong ministry, I had to agree with His Word.

So one day, He led me to write down the words that were to revolutionize my life and subsequently the lives of thousands of others who read this revelation. I called it "My Never Again List."

1. Never again will I confess "I can't," for *"I can do all things through Christ which strengtheneth me"* (Philippians 4:13).

2. Never again will I confess lack, for *"my God shall supply all [my] need according to his riches in glory by Christ Jesus"* (Philippians 4:19).

3. Never again will I confess fear, *"for God hath not given [me] the spirit of fear; but of power, and of love, and of a sound mind"* (2 Timothy 1:7).

4. Never again will I confess doubt and lack of faith, for *"God hath dealt to every man the measure of faith"* (Romans 12:3).

5.   Never again will I confess weakness, for *"the* LORD *is the strength of my life"* (Psalm 27:1) and *"the people that do know their God shall be strong, and do exploits"* (Daniel 11:32).

6.   Never again will I confess supremacy of Satan over my life, for *"greater is he that is in* [me], *than he that is in the world"* (1 John 4:4).

7.   Never again will I confess defeat, for *"God...always causeth* [me] *to triumph in Christ"* (2 Corinthians 2:14).

8.   Never again will I confess lack of wisdom, for I have *"Christ Jesus, who of God is made unto us wisdom"* (1 Corinthians 1:30).

9.   Never again will I confess sickness, for *"with his stripes* [I am] *healed"* (Isaiah 53:5) and Jesus *"Himself took* [my] *infirmities, and bare* [my] *sicknesses"* (Matthew 8:17).

10. Never again will I confess worries or frustrations, for I am *"casting all* [my] *care upon him; for he careth for* [me]*"* (1 Peter 5:7). In Christ, I am care-free!

11. Never again will I confess bondage, for *"where the Spirit of the* LORD *is, there is liberty"* (2 Corinthians 3:17). My body is a temple of the Holy Spirit!

12. Never again will I confess condemnation, for *"there is therefore now no condemnation to them which are in Christ Jesus"* (Romans 8:1). I am in Christ; therefore, I am free from condemnation.

19

THE TWO KINDS OF KNOWLEDGE

E. W. KENYON

One of the recent discoveries in our spiritual laboratory has been that there are two kinds of knowledge—sense knowledge and revelation knowledge.

The knowledge that our schools, colleges, and universities teach has come to us through the five senses. It is safe to say that there is no knowledge of chemistry, biology, metallurgy, mechanics, or any other field of research but that which has come to us through the five senses—seeing, tasting, hearing, smelling, and feeling. Our bodies have really been the laboratory in which the research has steadily gone on through the ages.

That knowledge is limited. It cannot find the human spirit. It cannot discover how the mind functions in the physical brain. It cannot find God or discover the origin of matter, life, force, or creation. All that it can discover are things it can see, taste, hear, smell, or feel. That's why we call it "sense knowledge."

Then there is another kind of knowledge called "revelation knowledge," which has come to us through the Bible. Revelation knowledge brings us in contact with the Creator and explains the "why" of creation, the reason for man, the nature of man, and the ultimate goal of man. It deals with things that the senses cannot discover or know by itself.

The unhappy fact is that sense knowledge has gained supremacy in the church, a spiritual organization, a spiritual body, that is to be governed through the Spirit instead of through the senses. When sense knowledge gained the ascendancy in the church and in the fountain of the church, the theological school, the church ceased to be a spiritual body and simply became a body of men governed by sense knowledge.

You can see why sense knowledge, which cannot understand spiritual things, will deny miracles, answers to prayer, and the very deity of Jesus, discrediting His resurrection and miracles. It is to be expected that sense knowledge will deny the miraculous, because it cannot explain or understand it.

The chief quest of sense knowledge is to find reality—man's spirit craves it—but it cannot be found by the senses. It is only discovered by the spirit. Sense knowledge has sent forth men called philosophers, who search after reality.

It is a profound fact, worthy of every man's consideration, that the man who really knows Jesus Christ, who has received eternal life, never turns to philosophy. If he has been a philosopher, he gives it up because he has arrived at reality in Christ.

Jesus said, "I am the way, the reality, and the life." (See John 14:6.) Jesus, then, is the answer to all true philosophy.[3]

---

3. If you wish to further study this subject, consult my little book *The Two Kinds of Knowledge.*

20

THE BOOK OF MIRACLES

DON GOSSETT

The Bible is a record of miracles. Its story of creation is a series of reason-staggering miracles. Every great achievement and every step in advance for the human race as recorded in the Bible has been a miracle.

As the Israelites walked in the presence of miracles, they progressed and built up their nation. When they resorted to reason, they fell prey to their enemies and were carried into captivity. As long as the Israelites walked in fellowship with God and kept their miracle covenant, they remained independent, a leader among the nations of the earth.

Furthermore, Jesus, the Incarnate One, was conceived in a miraculous way. His birth was attended by miracles, and His whole life was a series of miracles climaxing in the miracle of the ages—His death on the cross, His resurrection from the dead, and His ascension in the presence of five hundred witnesses. Jesus was a miracle from all angles. He was a greater miracle than any miracle He performed, because He was the miracle of God manifested in the flesh.

You say it is not reasonable. I know it is not. Miracles are not reasonable, but they happen. They are above reason. They belong to the realm of God and the realm of your spirit and mine.

The church was born in a miracle; it was fostered and developed and anchored in the heathen world by miracle. When philosophy took the place of miracles, Christianity became a religion; but wherever faith dominates, miracles take place. Wherever a body of people begins to walk with God, believe the Word and obey it, miracles follow. They must follow. You cannot have God in your midst without His manifesting Himself, and His manifestation is a miracle. Whenever an individual or a company of people dare to honor the Lord and to walk with Him, miracles take place.

21

THE FATHER HAS NO FAVORITES

E. W. KENYON

It was a great comfort to my heart when I realized that the Father has no favorites and that all the children have their own place in His heart. He loves each one of them even as He loves the Lord Jesus. Jesus said, *"That the world may know that thou…lovedst them, even as thou lovedst me"* (John 17:23 ASV).

We all have the same redemption. The work that the Father wrought in Christ absolutely destroyed the power of the enemy, and now redeems every person who accepts Christ as Savior and confess Him as Lord. We are redeemed from the works of the adversary and his dominion over our lives.

Everyone has the same righteousness. No one has a better righteousness or is more righteous. Righteousness comes through the new creation. When we are born again, we receive the life and nature of God, the Father. His nature makes us righteous, and no one has more of it than another.

All who receive His nature have come into the family and are recognized as the sons and daughters of the great Father-God.

Everyone has the same rights in the family. Though a man may have a different gift than another, he is not any dearer to the heart of the Father.

Furthermore, everyone has the same love nature, the same great Holy Spirit who raised Jesus from the dead. Each one has a right to the same kind of fellowship with the Father, to use the name of Jesus, and to use the authority invested in that name to deliver people from the dominion of Satan, to heal the sick, and to cast out demons.

The Father has no favorites. The closer your fellowship is with the Father, the sweeter and richer your life will be.

PART II:

HEALING IS NOW

22

"GOSH, SIR, ISN'T GOD WONDERFUL?"

DON GOSSETT

It happened in a town in northern British Columbia. In that town was a physician named Dr. Riley, who had emigrated from Ireland and was known as a good doctor; he was also known as an atheist. For years, Dr. Riley suffered with a painful rheumatic hip, which caused him to hobble when he walked.

In that same town lived a fifteen-year-old boy named Johnny Lake. Johnny was a devout Christian, and Dr. Riley took a liking to him. Often, the doctor took him on house calls with him.

One night, they were in the home of the Owens family. Seven-year-old Cathy Owens was dying with double pneumonia. As Dr. Riley listened to the girl gasp for every breath, he finally closed his black bag. Turning to Cathy's parents, he sadly informed them, "I'm sorry, but Cathy won't make it through the night. I must leave now to make other calls, but I'll return later. Meanwhile, I'll leave Johnny here to stay beside Cathy."

When Dr. Riley left the home, Johnny knelt beside Cathy's bed so he could speak softly into her ear. "God loves you, Cathy, and God is going to make you well," Johnny quietly whispered. "Breathe, Cathy, breathe. Oh, God, help Cathy to breathe."

Johnny continued, "Cathy, soon it will be spring. We'll go out on the lawn and make buttercups and daisy wheels. Breathe, Cathy, breathe. Oh, God, help Cathy to breathe.

"Then, Cathy, we'll look down a gopher hole and maybe we'll see a furry gopher. Breathe, Cathy, breathe. Oh, God, help Cathy to breathe!

"After that, Cathy, we'll go up on the bridge and watch the minnows in the river below, as the wagons go rolling across the bridge. Breathe, Cathy, breathe. Thank you, God. You are helping Cathy to breathe."

About two hours passed before Dr. Riley returned to the Owens' home. By this time, Johnny's speaking was no longer in a whisper but with vigor and excitement.

"How long has this been going on?" Dr. Riley asked the parents.

"Ever since you left, doctor," they replied. "There were times we thought Cathy was drawing her last breath. But now it seems she is getting stronger."

Dr. Riley took his stethoscope and examined Cathy. Without saying a word, a slow smile came upon his face.

Johnny jumped up and exclaimed, "God has healed Cathy, Dr. Riley! Gosh, sir, isn't God wonderful?"

Dr. Riley cautiously responded as he rose to his full height. As he placed his hand on his afflicted hip, he spoke that one name he had hated for so long—"God." He said, "God is wonderful! Yes, Johnny, God is wonderful." At that very moment, the severe pain departed from his hip.

That evening, Cathy Owens was miraculously healed of double pneumonia and Dr. Riley was totally healed of the rheumatic hip. Best of all, Dr. Riley became a deep believer in the living Christ as his Savior and Lord.

In Deuteronomy 30:19, God commands, *"I have set before you life and death…therefore choose life, that both thou and thy seed may live."*

The *Message* translation of Proverbs 18:21 is interesting: *"Words kill, words give life; they're either poison or fruit—you choose."*

Johnny Lake spoke words of life, words of faith, words of healing and blessing. When Dr. Riley broke a lifetime of rebellion by speaking the name "God," he, too, spoke words of life. Then his confession of the lordship of Jesus brought him salvation.

I challenge you: Choose life! Speak abundance instead of lack, strength instead of weakness, faith rather than doubt, victory in place of defeat, healing rather than sickness, freedom instead of condemnation.

You, too, can change the entire course of your life by bringing your tongue under the control of the Holy Spirit. God has given you the power to speak life or death through your tongue. There is awesome power in your tongue!

23

MUST JESUS BEAR OUR SINS AND DISEASES AGAIN?

E. W. KENYON

Jesus was made sin with our sins, for "[God] *hath made him to be sin for us, who knew no sin*" (2 Corinthians 5:21). "Surely, He has borne our sicknesses and carried our pains or diseases." (See Isaiah 53:4.)

I wonder if you have ever realized that when you ask the Father to heal you, you are asking Him to do something that He already did in Christ. When you ask someone to pray that your diseases may be healed, do you realize that you are repudiating Isaiah 53:4? You are counting it as though it had never been written. You are asking God to do again what He has already done for you.

When the intelligent person has done something wrong, he simply asks the Father to forgive him and to cleanse him from that unrighteous act. When the believer is sick, he should remember that sickness is a sin of the body, a sin of the sense, and look up and say, "Father, forgive me for this sin in my body, in my flesh."

When you grasp this truth, disease and sickness will not be such a formidable thing. You know that you have been healed and that healing is permanent, so if, in your ignorance, Satan brings disease upon you, all you need to do is confess it to God. Say, "Father, I am sorry that I permitted the adversary to touch my body, that holy thing, the temple of God. Now, in Jesus' name, I command the power of the adversary to be broken over it, and I take my perfect deliverance in Your name. Amen."

Healing is not a problem of faith as we understand that term, because that healing has already taken place; but there does come a time when His substitutionary sacrifice becomes a reality to you.

As long as you talk sickness and confess sickness, you will find the adversary taking advantage of your confession and making it a reality in your body.

Don't be afraid of a draft, thinking you are going to catch cold. I have not had a cold since I learned my place in Christ, since I learned to take it and act as though it were true.

You do not need to be sick, because by His stripes, you are healed. That work was wrought when Christ arose from the dead, and it belongs to you.

Now understand this fact. The Father does not say to you as a child, "Now, son/daughter, if you have faith in Me, I will heal you." Jesus talked like that to those Jews, those Old Covenant apostate men; but when He speaks to you, His son or daughter, He knows it is not a problem of faith on your part. That healing belongs to you. When you accepted Jesus, you accepted your healing.

So now, with quiet confidence, look up into your Father's face and thank Him for your perfect deliverance.

24

DON'T SAY YOU CAN'T WHEN GOD SAYS YOU CAN

DON GOSSETT

Mrs. Allison was suffering with an extreme case of long-standing asthma. I had prayed for her many times, but each time she'd seemed no better.

She approached me one day to tell me about her troubles. Deeply sincere but discouraged to the point that she could not talk to me without crying, she said, "Brother Gossett, I don't understand why I can't receive my healing. I know of other people you prayed for, people who suffered from asthma, and they have been healed. If it is true that God is no respecter of persons, why doesn't He heal me?"

I answered, "I don't know why you haven't received your healing, but go ahead and tell me all about yourself."

Immediately, she began to pour out her heart. She told me all about her illness and that she seemed unable to receive healing. "I have had this asthma for many years, but I can't be healed of it. I have been prayed for many times. Others besides you have prayed, but I can't get healed. Some nights, I have such a smothering attack of this asthma that I think I shall never be able to draw one more breath. The next day after such an attack, I can't even get out of bed. At other times, I am alright at the beginning of the day, but by noon the asthma will have started up again, and I simply can't do anything. I work in an office, and many days I can't finish my day's work because of my labored breathing and wheezing. I have prayed; I have fasted; I have searched my heart. Why can't I receive healing?"

I looked down at that woman. Everything about her showed her sincerity. She was obviously very earnestly seeking her healing from the Lord.

"Mrs. Allison," I began, "I want to help you, and I believe that Jesus wants to heal you. But there is something you must overcome, something just as serious as the asthma, before you can be healed."

Her puzzled expression seemed to be saying to me, "I don't understand what you're talking about. I have tried everything."

I didn't even wait for her to put that question into words. I spoke directly to her and to her problem. "If I point out something I feel is very important, can I be perfectly honest with you and give it to you straight? You know how much I want to help you. Will you take it from me, knowing that I'm only the Lord's servant?"

Without a moment's hesitation, she replied, "Oh, yes, I have come to you for the truth, and I want you to tell me the truth. Help me any way you can; if the Lord shows you anything about my life that's not as it should be, I want you to tell me. You won't hurt my feelings. Please tell me."

Quietly and slowly I explained to her, "It's true you have a serious case of asthma, but what I'm referring to is something just as serious, if not more serious, than the asthma—your negative attitude. You have the worst case of 'I can't-itus' I have ever witnessed. I have been listening to you, and no fewer than a dozen times you have said, 'I can't.' 'I can't be healed.' 'I can't get my breath.' 'I can't get out of bed in the morning.' 'I can't continue in the day.' 'I can't stay at the office.' Your life seems to be made up of 'I can't do this' and 'I can't do that.' Nowhere in the Bible does God describe you as an 'I can't-er.' Somehow, you have taken on this malady of 'I can't-itus.' Before you can expect any improvement in your life, any healing, you must change that 'I can't' to 'I can.' Until you do that, you cannot gain the attention of God to help you as He wishes to do."

The entire time I had been talking to her, Mrs. Allison had been crying. As moved as I was about her trouble and emotional condition, I knew that I must continue if I were to help her get the attention of God for His grace and power.

She accepted my comments and, still crying, asked me through tears, "But what can I do about it? How can I change my attitude?"

I opened my Bible to Philippians 4:13. I handed it to her and asked her to read what it said. Softly but with a determination I had not heard in her voice before, she read, *"I can do all things through Christ which strengtheneth me."*

"Now, that's the secret," I told her. "Instead of saying, 'I can't receive healing,' begin to affirm, 'Through Christ who strengthens me, I can do all things. I can receive my healing. I can be made completely whole through Christ, who is my Strength and my Healer. By His stripes, I am healed.'"

It was not an instant recovery. Mrs. Allison had practiced "I can't" for so long that it required real discipline for her to train her unruly lips to speak God's Word. Many months later, I saw her again. This time, she was joyful and bright. She eagerly shared with me her testimony of God's complete healing of the painful, frightening asthma.

How do you have faith? You decide to take God at His Word. How do you doubt? You decide not to take God at His Word.

When it comes to what you can do and have in Christ, don't say "I can't" when God says "You can!"

25

WORRY DESTROYS EFFICIENCY

E. W. KENYON

Worry is the unhealthy child of fear and unbelief. What children this married couple has begotten!

Worry leads to the waste of vital energy and disturbs our health systems, impairing our ability. And it becomes a mental disease. Almost everyone has it. It is contagious and leads to all kinds of physical and mental disorders.

But its cure is simple:

Trust in the Lord *with all thine heart; and lean not unto thine own understanding. In all thy ways acknowledge him, and he shall direct thy paths."* (Proverbs 3:5–6)

[Cast] *all your care* [anxiety] *upon him; for he careth for you."* (1 Peter 5:7)

Get quiet for a moment and remember this: God is on your side. If God is for you, who can be against you? (See Romans 8:31.)

People can't conquer the man who trusts in the Lord with all his heart. There aren't enough enemies in all the world to whip the man who trusts absolutely in the wisdom of God his Father and does not lean upon sense knowledge.

No man is safe to go out into the business world until he has first learned the secret of absolute trust in the Lord. So if you haven't learned it yet, and you are bearing your burdens and sickness with fretting and care and anxiety, go alone and settle the great issue with Him. Take His wisdom and grace to go out and do your work with perfect efficiency.

26

DOES GOD HEAL?

DON GOSSETT

Years ago, I heard about healing services being conducted in a church with positive results. I made an investigation among my friends about the subject of healing. Their views on the subject of healing varied. Some said, "God can heal, but He won't." Others said, "God can heal, and He might." But it was the dear people who embraced the full gospel of Jesus, who emphatically declared, "God can heal, and God will heal," who encouraged me.

When my mother and dad attended the meetings of evangelist William Freeman, when they sensed the great reality of the Lord's miracle-working power, they were fascinated. Surprisingly, they wanted to return—and they did. About the third night, my mother went forward to receive the Savior. It was a wonderful miracle when my own sweet mother accepted the Lord and was born again of the Spirit.

The next night, my mother was in the prayer line. When Brother Freeman prayed for her in Jesus' name, the power of the Lord swept through her afflicted body and in a moment made her every whit whole. It was a beautiful miracle that greatly affected my family. When they saw how real Jesus was, and how He manifested His loving concern for suffering humanity, my family was all eager to accept the Lord. And they did.

I will never forget the night my mother and dad returned home from those meetings and I met them about midnight. They walked in the door, glanced at each other with a smile, and then my mother broke the news: "Dad was saved tonight!" Praise the Lord!

We had a hallelujah time that night, rejoicing in the fact that both my mother and dad were saved by the grace of God, heaven-born and heaven-bound. Never again did my dad partake of the impurities that had characterized his life for almost forty-five years. Drinking, gambling, unfaithfulness to the marriage vows— these were all things of the past. Indeed, *"old things are passed away;...all things are become new"* (2 Corinthians 5:17) when Jesus Christ makes someone a new creature.

27

GOD'S METHOD OF HEALING BABES IN CHRIST

E. W. KENYON

"Is any among you sick?" There should be no sick among you because "by his stripes you are healed." Because there has been no spiritual development or growth, and you are still babes in Christ, you are sick."
—*Healing for the Carnally Minded Man*

Carnal means "sense-ruled." The carnally minded man is a Christian who has not yet come to the place where the Word rules him and governs his thinking. He is called a "babe in Christ"—carnally minded, fleshly. He is ruled by the flesh, by what he sees with his eyes, by what he feels, hears, tastes, and smells. He is a body-ruled, sense-governed child of God. He is a babe in Christ.

Paul said, "*And, I, brethren, could not speak unto you as unto spiritual*" (1 Corinthians 3:1 ASV); that is, Paul could not speak to men whose spirits had gained the ascendancy over their thinking. Their spirit had been recreated, but their unrenewed mind ruled their spirit. "I cannot speak unto you as men whose minds are subordinate to the Word of God." Their minds were not renewed. They were still babes.

> *Of whom we have many things to say, and hard of interpreta-*
> *tion, seeing ye are become dull of hearing....For every one that*
> *partaketh of milk is without experience of the word of right-*
> *eousness; for he is a babe.*　　　(Hebrews 5:11, 13 ASV)

How many believers fall under this admonition. They cannot understand the Word. This *"word of righteousness"* is very little understood. They have never had an experience in living right-eousness. What do we mean by that?

Righteousness means the ability to stand in the presence of the Father, or of demons, or of sickness and disease, without the sense of inferiority, condemnation, or sin-consciousness.

Those who live righteousness, or who know by the Word that they are the righteousness of God in Christ, are absolute masters over circumstances, demons, and disease.

> *Him who knew no sin he made to be sin on our behalf; that we*
> *might become the righteousness of God in him.*
> 　　　　　　　　　　　　　(2 Corinthians 5:21 ASV)

You are having experience in the Word of righteousness. You are finding that it is the Word that heals.

This ministry of the Word of God is the Word of righteous-ness. It is the Word of righteousness that sets men free, leads them out of Satan's dominion into the liberty and freedom of the sons of God. How fearless they become. How mightily they speak.

> *But solid food is for fullgrown.men, even those who by reason*
> *of use have their senses exercised to discern good and evil.*
> 　　　　　　　　　　　　　　(Hebrews 5:14 asv)

The believer described above has grown up into a spiritual life in Christ. He has fed on the Word until the Word transfigured him. James 5:14–16 (ASV) is God's method of healing the carnally minded, or the babes in Christ. God, in great grace, says,

> *Let him call for the elders of the church; and let them pray over him, anointing him with oil in the name of the Lord: and the prayer of faith shall save him that is sick, and the Lord shall raise him up; and if he have committed sins, it shall be forgiven him. Confess therefore your sins one to another, and pray one for another, that ye may be healed. The supplication of a righteous man availeth much in its working.*

Notice very carefully these facts. This man cannot see that his disease was laid on Christ, but he can see the elders, hear their prayers, and feel their hands and the anointing oil upon his forehead. He is living in the realm of the senses, when grace comes down and meets him in this realm.

If he had taken advantage of his privileges, he would have acted on 1 John 1:9 (ASV): *"If we confess our sins, he is faithful and righteous to forgive us our sins, and to cleanse us from all unrighteousness."*

This Scripture is for the Christian. Had that believer, that babe in Christ, taken advantage of his rights and privileges, he would have looked up and said, "Father, forgive me for the thing I have done, which caused my sickness." And then the Father would have forgiven him and healed him. But he has to see and feel before he can believe. He belongs to Thomas' class: "When I see, I will believe." (See John 20:25.)

Practically all the faith that men had in Jesus before His death and resurrection was sense knowledge faith. They believed in things they saw and heard. They could not believe in a resurrection, because they had never seen a resurrection. They had seen Lazarus raised from the dead; but he was simply raised, brought back to life again. He was not resurrected, for he died again.

Oh, the grace of our Lord Jesus Christ that comes down to our level and meets us where we are—even when we apparently cannot act on the Word, because we are governed by the senses.

THE ALPHABET OF HEALING

DON GOSSETT

Read and memorize the following miracle-producing Scriptures. They will bring complete healing to you!

a. *"**Attend** to my words; incline thine ear unto my sayings. Let them not depart from thine eyes; keep them in the midst of thine heart. For they are life unto those that find them, and health to all their flesh"* (Proverbs 4:20–22).

b. *"**Beloved**, I wish above all things that thou mayest prosper and be in health, even as thy soul prospereth"* (3 John 2).

c. *"**Create** in me a clean heart, O God; and renew a right spirit within me"* (Psalm 51:10).

d. *"**Deal** bountifully with thy servant, that I may live, and keep thy word"* (Psalm 119:17).

e. *"**Effectual** fervent prayer of a righteous man availeth much"* (James 5:16).

f. *"**Forget** not all [the Lord's] benefits…who healeth all thy diseases"* (Psalm 103:2–3).

g. "*God* anointed Jesus of Nazareth with the Holy Ghost and with power: who went about doing good, and healing all that were oppressed of the devil; for God was with him" (Acts 10:38).

h. "*Himself* took our infirmities, and bare our sicknesses" (Matthew 8:17).

i. "*I am the* LORD *that healeth thee*" (Exodus 15:26).

j. "*Jesus* Christ the same yesterday, and to day, and for ever" (Hebrews 13:8).

k. "*Know* ye not that your body is the temple of the Holy Ghost which is in you, which ye have of God, and ye are not your own? For ye are bought with a price: therefore glorify God in your body, and in your spirit, which are God's" (1 Corinthians 6:19–20).

l. "*Lay* hands on the sick, and they shall recover" (Mark 16:18).

m. "*Merry* heart doeth good like a medicine: but a broken spirit drieth the bones" (Proverbs 17:22).

n. "*Name* through faith in his name hath made this man strong, whom ye see and know: yea, the faith which is by him hath given him this perfect soundness in the presence of you all" (Acts 3:16).

o. "*Ought* not this woman, being a daughter of Abraham, whom Satan hath bound, lo, these eighteen years, be loosed from this bond...?" (Luke 13:16).

p. "*Power* of the Lord was present to heal them" (Luke 5:17).

q. "*Quicken* your mortal bodies by his Spirit that dwelleth in you" (Romans 8:11).

r. "*Resist* the devil, and he will flee from you" (James 4:7).

s. "*Sent* his word, and healed them" (Psalm 107:20).

t. *"Talk ye of all his wondrous works"* (Psalm 105:2).

u. *"Unto you that fear my name shall the Sun of righteousness arise with healing in his wings"* (Malachi 4:2).

v. *"Virtue* [went] *out of him, and healed them all"* (Luke 6:19).

w. *"With his stripes we are healed"* (Isaiah 53:5).

x. *"Expectation is from him"* (Psalm 62:5).

y. *"Youth is renewed like the eagle's"* (Psalm 103:5).

z. *"Zealous of spiritual gifts"* (1 Corinthians 14:12).

29

METHODS OF HEALING

E. W. KENYON

There are five ways by which healings are obtained through the Word. The first method is simply using healing as a means of advertising the gospel as well as blessing the people. John 14:13–14 (ASV) can be used in this connection.

> *And whatsoever ye shall ask [or demand] in my name, that will I do, that the Father may be glorified in the Son. If ye shall ask anything in my name, that will I do.*

If a pain comes, you say, "In the name of Jesus Christ, leave my body." Then the pain must go. You are the master of your own body. You rule it. You have a right to freedom from pain or sickness. So in Jesus' name, you can command sickness to leave. You are not demanding it of the Father, because the Father has given you authority over these demoniacal forces.

Furthermore, you can use the name to break the power of the adversary over the unsaved and make it easy for them to accept Christ. In that name, "*them that believe...shall lay hands on the sick, and they shall recover"* (Mark 16:17–18). Every believer should understand this clearly, that he has a right to perfect deliverance from the hand of his enemy in that name.

A second method is found in this same verse: *"In my name… they shall lay hands on the sick, and they shall recover"* (Mark 16:17–18). The believer has the nature and life of God in him. The Spirit dwells in him. It is that power within him that goes out through his hands and heals the sick in the name of Jesus.

Sometimes, it is accompanied by manifestations. The person feels the life of God pouring through his body. But other times, there is no manifestation. It makes no difference whether or not there is any sense witness. The same power that is in the believer can be exercised in the name of Jesus for a sick one in a distant place. The moment he prays in that name, God's healing power reaches out to that person and he is healed.

A third method is for the carnal believer, that is, the believer who is governed by the senses and not by the Word. Remember, Scripture calls him a babe in Christ. (See 1 Corinthians 3:1.) James says,

> Is any among you sick? Let him call for the elders of the church; and let them pray over him, anointing him with oil in the name of the Lord: and the prayer of faith shall save him that is sick, and the Lord shall raise him up; and if he have committed sins, it shall be forgiven him.
>
> (James 5:14–15 ASV)

This Scripture is not for full-grown believers but for those who have never developed their spiritual life so as to take their places in Christ. It is for those who must depend on others to pray for them.

A fourth method of healing is found in the book of John.

> And in that day ye shall ask me no question. Verily, verily, I say unto you, if ye shall ask anything of the Father, he will

give it you in my name. Hitherto have ye asked nothing in my name: ask, and ye shall receive, that your joy may be made full. (John 16:23–24 ASV)

Every believer has a right to ask the Father for healing or any other blessing; and if he asks in the name of Jesus, he has an absolute guarantee that the Father will hear and answer his petition.

A fifth method of healing is found in Matthew 18:19–20 (ASV).

If two of you shall agree on earth as touching anything that they shall ask, it shall be done for them of my Father who is in heaven. For where two or three are gathered together in my name, there am I in the midst of them.

When two are united in prayer, demanding in Jesus' name the healing of loved ones, they are bound to be answered. God watches over His Word to make it good.

There is another method of healing which I believe to be the best. Scripture says,

Surely he hath borne our griefs, and carried our sorrows; yet we did esteem him stricken, smitten of God, and afflicted. But he was wounded for our transgressions, he was bruised for our iniquities; the chastisement of our peace was upon him; and with his stripes we are healed. (Isaiah 53:4–5 ASV)

Here is the absolute statement of fact that by His stripes, we are healed:

Who his own self bare our sins in his body upon the tree, that we, having died unto sins, might live unto righteousness; by whose stripes ye were healed. (1 Peter 2:24 ASV)

That it might be fulfilled which was spoken through Isaiah the prophet, saying: Himself took our infirmities, and bare our diseases. (Matthew 8:17 ASV)

These Scriptures prove that healing is ours. We simply know that by His stripes, we are healed. We thank the Father for our perfect deliverance. It is not necessary that we pray or ask the Father to heal us, because we know that He said, *"By His stripes ye were healed"* (Isaiah 53:5). The afflictions in our bodies were laid upon Jesus. He bore them. We do not need to bear them.

All we need to do is to recognize and accept that fact. We refuse to allow disease in our bodies, because we are healed. Every believer should thoroughly understand that his own healing was consummated in Christ. This would mean the end of chronic troubles in the body of the believer!

30

GREAT JOY IN HEALING

DON GOSSETT

When I first launched into full-time gospel ministry, I was living at the home of some friends. One day, I was playing with their five-year-old son, who persistently begged me to hold his arms and swing him around. Picking him up, I felt his little bones break in my strong hand. His parents were terrified. They rushed him to the doctor in the small nearby town, and a doctor took X-rays and came out with a disheartening diagnosis: "The boy's arm has been so badly broken that major surgery will be required to reset the bones. I am not equipped to perform that operation here; I will call the nearest hospital and request that they prepare for surgery."

We rushed the boy to this hospital fifty miles away. He was seated between his parents in the front seat, and I was alone in the backseat. I felt sick at heart to think that this little fellow was facing surgery and that I had actually broken his arm! Aware of the gravity of the condition, I took my New Testament out from my pocket and opened it to John 16:24: *"Hitherto have ye asked nothing in my name: ask, and ye shall receive, that your joy may be full*"!

With tears in my eyes, I prayed, "Lord, what full joy it would bring us if You healed this boy's broken arm, even as we journey now. In the name of Jesus, I ask You to heal this arm and make it every whit whole!" That was a most earnest prayer. The boy soon fell asleep for the rest of the trip.

When we arrived, the doctors were ready for surgery. First, however, they needed to take more X-rays to determine how to operate. In about fifteen minutes, they returned with baffled expressions. They showed us the X-rays, and there was no indication of any broken bones!

While these fine physicians were astonished, we had fullness of joy that Jesus had miraculously intervened and healed the boy's broken arm! Hallelujah! What jubilation we had! How we thanked our triumphant Christ!

The LORD hath done great things for us; whereof we are glad.

(Psalm 126:3)

31

HEALING IN REDEMPTION

E. W. KENYON

We have seen healing for the world in the name of Jesus. Now let us see healing for the man who enjoys the fullness of his privileges in Christ.

Isaiah 53 is a preview of Jesus' public ministry and His substitutionary sacrifice. It is a veiled prophecy, but it is revealed now through the Pauline revelation as belonging to us.

> He was despised, and rejected of men; a man of sorrows [pains], and acquainted with grief [disease].
>
> (Isaiah 53:3 ASV)

He was a root out of dry ground. But He was precious to the Father, though condemned by the world.

> As one from whom men hide their face he was despised; and we esteemed him not. Surely he hath borne our griefs [sicknesses], and carried our sorrows [diseases]; yet we did esteem him stricken, smitten of God, and afflicted.
>
> (Isaiah 53:3–4 ASV)

Like as many were astonished at thee (his visage was so marred more than any man, and his form more than the sons of men). (Isaiah 52:14 ASV)

The margin of *The Cross-Reference Bible* reads, "[Men] were dumbfounded at him, for deformed was his appearance so as not to be a man, and his figure so as not to be human." It continues, "So shall many be amazed over Him. His visage was so marred unlike to a man, and His form unlike to the sons of men....[His visage was] so as not to be a man, and his figure no more resembled man."

He was made sin with our sin and was under the dominion of Satan. This is a description of Jesus' Spirit, not His body. He was made sick with our diseases, and when those diseases came upon His precious Spirit, He no longer resembled a man.

The heart cannot take it in. Reason stands dumb in the presence of statements like these. "He was *'stricken, smitten of God, and afflicted'*" (Isaiah 53:4 ASV).

It was God who laid our diseases upon Him. It was justice that demanded a recompense for our offenses. *"He was wounded for our transgressions, he was bruised for our iniquities; the chastisement of our peace was upon him; and with his stripes we are healed"* (Isaiah 53:5 ASV).

SICKNESS IS SPIRITUAL

Now you can see that sickness was healed spiritually. God did not deal with sickness physically.

Disease today is spiritual. I have found that when I can prove, through the Word, that our diseases were laid on Jesus to a sick man, and he accepts that fact, he is instantly healed.

As long as we think that disease is purely physical, we will not get our deliverance. But when we know it is spiritual, and it must be healed by the Word of God—for you remember that He said, *"He sent his word, and healed them"* (Psalm 107:20)—then healing becomes a reality. *"He was wounded for our transgressions"*—this was spiritual. *"He was bruised for our iniquities"*—this was a spiritual bruising.

The wounds that the soldiers made did not take away sin, for if they had, sin would be a physical thing, a sense knowledge thing. Human justice deals only with sense evidences—not what a man thinks but what he says or does. No, Jesus endured sufferings that the senses cannot understand. They stand mute and helpless in the presence of this great spiritual tragedy that took place on Calvary. It was not the physical wounds made by the lictor. It was the stripes that justice laid upon His spirit.

> *All we like sheep have gone astray; we have turned every one to his own way; and Jehovah hath laid on him the iniquity of us all.*   (Isaiah 53:6 asv)

> *Yet it pleased Jehovah to bruise him; he hath made him sick.*
>   (rv marginal rendering)

Love could see humanity redeemed. Faith could see a new creation. God made Christ sick with our sickness. We need not be sick. Only ignorance of our rights or refusal to act upon the Word can keep us ill. He made Him sin with our sin. We need not remain in sin. He became sin that we might become righteous. He went to hell so that we might go to heaven. He was made weak that we might be made strong. He took our place, met every need, satisfied every claim of justice, and set us free.

If this be the case, sickness on the part of the believer is wrong, just as weakness and every other thing that Satan brought upon man is wrong, because Christ has already suffered to put it away.

SOME FACTS ABOUT THE SUPERNATURAL LIFE

In the mind of the Father, we are supermen. We are conquerors and overcomers.

For whatsoever is begotten of God overcometh the world: and this is the victory that hath overcome the world, even our faith. And who is he that overcometh the world, but he that believeth that Jesus is the Son of God? (1 John 5:4–5 ASV)

It was our faith that brought us into the family of conquerors. We believe that Jesus is the Son of God, that He died for our sins according to Scripture, and that He arose again for our justification. We believe that the moment we take Him to be our Savior and confess Him as our Lord, God takes us to be His children and gives us eternal life.

This places us in the realm of conquerors. We are supermen and superwomen. Healing and victory are ours. They are ours without asking. All we need to do is to simply know it and praise Him for it.

Having then a great high priest, who hath passed through the heavens, Jesus the Son of God, let us hold fast our confession.
(Hebrews 4:14 ASV)

The King James Version reads, "*profession.*" We are to hold fast our confession. What is our confession? It is that we are new creations, that sin has been put away, and that we are the righteousness of God in Him. We confess, "Surely He has borne our sicknesses and carried our diseases." (See Isaiah 53:4.) Our confession is that He was stricken, smitten of God with our infirmities and weaknesses, and now by His stripes we are absolutely healed. Sin and disease have been put away, and in the name of Jesus, we have dominion over Satan and the work of his hands.

In His name, we cast out demons. In His name, we lay hands on the sick and they recover. If we can cast out demons, we can also command the demon "Disease" to leave our bodies, for disease was brought by a demon and is being developed by a demon. We say, "In Jesus' name, Disease, leave this body." That demon is under obligation to the name of Jesus to obey.

When Jesus arose from the dead, He arose because He (and we!) had conquered Satan.

> *Having despoiled the principalities and the powers, he made a show of them openly, triumphing over them in it.*
>
> (Colossians 2:15 ASV)

Jesus' triumph is our triumph. Jesus' victory is our victory. He did nothing for Himself; it was all for us. Today we are more than conquerors through Him, who loved us.

We should never talk about our diseases. When we tell our troubles to people, it is always to get their sympathy. That trouble came from the adversary. When we tell our troubles, we are giving our testimony of Satan's ability to get us into difficulty. When we talk about our diseases, we are glorifying the adversary, who had the ability to put that disease upon us. When we confess our lack of strength or ability, we confess that Satan has so blinded us that we cannot enjoy our rights and privileges.

The prayer of unbelief never gives faith. When you pray for faith, you confess your unbelief. This increases your doubts, for the prayer is never heard. The doubter often prays for other things already his own. God has blessed him with every spiritual blessing that governs every spiritual need. Redemption has never been seen as a reality to him. It is a theory, a creed, a doctrine. He expects experimental evidence of it.

Satan takes advantage of our ignorance of redemption and puts disease upon us, holding us in bondage. The defeated one holds his master, the believer, in bondage.

Jehovah is my light and my salvation; whom shall I fear?
Jehovah is the strength of my life; of whom shall I be afraid?
(Psalm 27:1 ASV)

God has made Christ to be wisdom unto us. He has made Him to be redemption unto us. If this be true, then Satan has no right to reign over us with sickness, disease, weakness, or failure.

Every time we talk of our troubles, we glorify the being who put the troubles upon us. Our confession should be that God is today our Strength, our Wisdom, our complete and perfect Redemption, our Sanctification, and our Righteousness. We are the righteousness of God in Him. We can do all things in Him who strengthens us.

Today, the name of Jesus on our lips can conquer disease and sickness. That name can bring courage and victory to the defeated and the whipped.

32

HOW TO STAY SICK

DON GOSSETT

Here are some ways to stay sick; avoid them at all cost!

1. Tell others in great detail about your infirmities. This will not only bring sympathy and attention; it will also give you a good conversation piece and discourage the faith of others who may need to trust God for healing and health.

2. Speak like this: "When it comes to healing, I'm a real doubting Thomas; I have to be shown before I will ever believe." Or, "It's so hard to believe God these days. I have such little faith. I've tried trusting God, but it just doesn't work."

3. Here's another key phrase that will help you stay sick: "I must be like the apostle Paul; I must have a thorn in the flesh. Paul prayed thrice for it to be removed, but his request was denied. So my infirmity must be my thorn in the flesh." (Note: Paul's thorn in the flesh was a

messenger from Satan sent to buffet him because of the abundance of revelation that God had given him.)

4. Tune into an actual conversation of someone who stays sick much of the time, and you'll gain tips on how to acquire the same results. For example, such people say, "All I know about what the Bible says about healing is Paul's thorn in the flesh, Job's boils, and Timothy's sore stomach. And the time when Paul left one of his helpers behind sick. Now if healing was to be, surely a great man like Paul would have been able to bring it."

5. If you want to stay sick, here's a list of what *never* to say: Never confess, "By His stripes, I am healed." (See Isaiah 53:5; 1 Peter 2:24.) This would boldly honor what Jesus Christ provided when He was striped for the healing of His people. Never confess, *"Himself took our infirmities, and bare our sicknesses"* (Matthew 8:17). If you said this, you'd be agreeing with God, and this would not help you stay sick. When you talk this way, you bring honor and glory to the dear Son of God, who suffered such punishment that you might be healed. Never say, *"Jesus Christ the same yesterday, and to day, and for ever"* (Hebrews 13:8). This would be admitting that the same Christ who healed the sick when He walked the shores of Galilee is still the same today in His compassion, power, and willingness to heal. This will not do if you want to stay sick!

6. Often tell others about your operations, afflictions, and health problems in general. This will distinguish you as one who's really "lived" and will keep you on the level of natural living rather than supernatural living that Christ came to give: *"I am come that they might have life, and that they might have it more abundantly"* (John 10:10).

7. If you have ever received healing or a miraculous answer to prayer, don't talk about it. This may cause you to think that God might do it again and that you would be sick no longer. Specialize in telling others about those who supposedly "died trusting God." Say, "I knew a dear saint of God, a real Christian, and if God wouldn't heal a wonderful Christian like him, there is no hope for me."

8. If one of your loved ones or relatives has died of some disease, talk about it often. Say, "I had faith in God for a long time, but when He wouldn't heal my loved one, then I just lost all faith for healing." Be bitter against God.

9. Every time you hear a wonderful testimony of healing on the radio or TV, or read about one, be sure to scoff and cast doubt upon its authenticity. Declare that there was probably an error in diagnosis or something to discredit what God has done.

10. Always say, "I can't get my healing. God just won't meet my need. I'm afraid I'd better do something else than try to trust in God. I'm so weak in my faith. Satan is so powerful, and he's the awful oppressor. I've tried before but was defeated. I worry so much whether this condition is cancer. It seems that I'm destined to remain in physical bondage. I've had everybody pray for me but haven't gotten any results. My faith is shattered. Why should I praise the Lord? I'm so despondent."

If you want to stay sick, just practice these ten steps. If you are "sick and tired of being sick and tired," then confess just the opposite, and you'll obtain the benefits. What you confess is exactly what you'll possess, whether sickness or health!

33

MADE WELL IN CHRIST

E. W. KENYON

No matter how you look at Christianity, it is a miracle, and the most amazing miracle is the new creation. We have never been able to get to the heart of it; we have stood outside as spectators and looked at it from its various angles. Let's look at it now.

A man becomes a new creation by receiving the very life and nature of God. Take this Scripture as an illustration:

> Buried with him in baptism, wherein ye were also raised with him through the faith in the working of God, who raised him from the dead. And you, being dead through your trespasses and the uncircumcision of your flesh, you, I say, did he make alive together with him, having forgiven us all our trespasses.
>
> (Colossians 2:12–13 ASV)

We have been made alive together with Him. We were raised *"with him through the faith in the working of God"*—this is the legal aspect of the new creation. Everything that is legally ours can become a vital reality.

In the mind of the Father, we were made alive with Christ. When He was made alive in Spirit, we were made alive in Spirit. This becomes a reality to us when we personally accept Christ as Savior and confess Him as Lord. The life of God comes into our spirits and recreates us.

> *And you did he make alive, when ye were dead through your trespasses and sins.*   (Ephesians 2:1 ASV)

This can be called the miracle of Christianity—becoming an actual new creation.

If we did not fear old age, there would be more pleasure in it than in youth. We dread it because of the haunting fear of pain and disease and the struggle with death.

A few facts about life and death may be helpful to us. First, spiritual death is the parent of physical death. There was no physical death until Adam died spiritually.

There was no death in the original blueprints of creation. We know that at the end of this age, death will be swallowed up in immortality. Scripture says, *"The last enemy that shall be abolished is death"* (1 Corinthians 15:26 ASV).

There is going to be a deathless eternity. Why can't there be a sickless present? I believe it is the will of the Father that the church be as free from sickness as it is from sin.

Death is an enemy, and weakness and disease are enemies. Now death is not only the enemy of man; it is also the enemy of God.

In the resurrection of the Lord Jesus, death lost its dominion:

> *But hath now been manifested by the appearing of our Saviour Christ Jesus, who abolished death, and brought life and immortality to light through the gospel.*
>
>   (2 Timothy 1:10 ASV)

The Lord Jesus did two things: He abolished the dominion of death, and He brought life and immortality to us. When He arose from the dead, He had personally conquered death. He also had conquered death in Lazarus and in the widow's son. He was the Lord of life.

> *And death and Hades were cast into the lake of fire.*
>   (Revelation 20:14 ASV)

> *And he shall wipe away every tear from their eyes; and death shall be no more; neither shall there be mourning, nor crying, nor pain, any more.*   (Revelation 21:4 ASV)

When He returns, it will be the end of death. This promise of the final destruction of death suggests that in the plan of redemption is something to give us assurance of a sickless life, until our bodies wear out and mortality wins without a struggle.

> *He was despised, and rejected of men; a man of sorrows, and acquainted with grief: and as one from whom men hide their face he was despised; and we esteemed him not. Surely he hath borne our griefs, and carried our sorrows; yet we did esteem him stricken, smitten of God, and afflicted. But he was wounded for our transgressions, he was bruised for our iniquities; the chastisement of our peace was upon him; and with his stripes we are healed.*   (Isaiah 53:3–5 ASV)

> *Yet it pleased Jehovah to bruise him; he hath put him to grief ["made him sick" (Young's Literal Translation)].*
>   (Isaiah 53:10 ASV)

> *Because he hath poured out his soul unto death: and he was numbered with the transgressors: and he bare the sin of many, and made intercession for the transgressors.*   (Isaiah 53:12)

That is His high priestly ministry now at the right hand of the Father. We can see in this whole program that heads up in the words *"with his stripes we are healed"* that the sin and disease problems have been settled.

As surely as Jesus was our sin substitute, so surely have we become the righteousness of God in Him. (See 2 Corinthians 5:21.) And the object of His being made sick with our diseases was that we might be perfectly healed with His life. There is no escaping the fact that as surely as He dealt with the sin problem, He dealt with the disease problem.

> *But now once at the end of the ages hath he been manifested to put away sin by the sacrifice of himself.* (Hebrews 9:26 ASV)

> *But he, when he had offered one sacrifice for sins for ever, sat down on the right hand of God.*   (Hebrews 10:12 ASV)

He put sin away that we might be born again, become new creations, that the sin nature which had held us in bondage to the adversary should be eradicated and that the nature of God should take its place.

It is the new nature that settles the sin problem for each of us individually. The problem of sin is settled. The things we did before we accepted Christ are wiped out as though they had never been.

Now we are in the family. We are the righteousness of God in Him. Hebrews 10:38 (ASV) says, *"But my righteous one shall live by faith: and if he shrink back, my soul hath no pleasure in him."* The new creation is called the righteousness of God. His standing with the Father is just like Jesus' standing. And if he sins, he has an Advocate with the Father, Jesus Christ the righteous. He loses the sense of righteousness when he sins, but Jesus, the Righteous One, intercedes for him and restores his lost fellowship and sense of righteousness.

When a man confesses his sin to the Father, he is forgiven:

If we confess our sins, he is faithful and righteous to forgive us our sins, and to cleanse us from all unrighteousness.

(1 John 1:9 ASV)

This restores his spiritual fellowship with the Father, bringing him back into full communion with Him.

Now, in the mind of God, he is just as much healed of disease as he is healed of sin, for *"by his stripes we are healed."* Diseases of the spirit—doubts, fears, sin-consciousness, a sense of inferiority, fear of unworthiness, and a sense of unfitness to stand in God's presence—are what keeps a person from healing. But the blood of Jesus Christ, God's Son, cleanses from all this, the moment a man acknowledges his sin. Forgiveness means the absolute wiping out of everything he has confessed, as though he had never committed the act.

For indeed we that are in this tabernacle do groan, being burdened; not for that we would be unclothed, but that we would be clothed upon, that what is mortal may be swallowed up of life. Now he that wrought us for this very thing is God, who gave unto us the earnest of the Spirit.

(2 Corinthians 5:4–5 ASV)

The Greek word here for life is *"zoe."* It means eternal life, or resurrection life. In other words, it means that the life of the Son of God, eternal life, can absolutely dominate, rule, swallow up, and control our physical lives.

Furthermore, if, after we have been healed of disease, the adversary puts upon us some other disease or infirmity, which breaks our physical fellowship with the Father, all we need to do to be healed is to follow the procedure that we followed when we broke spiritual fellowship with the Father—confessing our sins.

If this be true, then sickness is absolutely defeated, physical weakness is eliminated, and Psalm 27:1 (ASV) is a reality:

Jehovah is my light and my salvation; whom shall I fear? Jehovah is the strength of my life; of whom shall I be afraid?

So is John 8:12 (ASV):

[Jesus said,] *I am the light of the world: he that followeth me shall not walk in the darkness, but shall have the light of life.*

Light is knowledge, and Jesus is the Light of the World. So he who walks in that Light will not stumble as one who walks in darkness, because he will have the Light of life.

Thy word is a lamp unto my feet, and light unto my path.
(Psalm 119:105 ASV)

The Word will be his lamp, his light, and his salvation. This is redemption; this is deliverance from the things that are not in the Father's will. You cannot for a moment believe that mortality—weakness, sickness, and death—is in the will of the Father. You cannot conceive of disease and sickness as being the will of the Father. *"Jehovah is my light and my salvation"*—this means salvation from sickness, disease, and weakness of the physical body.

Redemption planned this very thing—that these bodies of ours should never be subject to disease after we are born again. Fear of weakness, death, or pain no longer dominates our lives, because we are delivered. We are conquerors.

Someone may ask, "What about Paul's thorn in the flesh?" That was not sickness. It was a demon interfering with his public ministry and speech, making him stammer. It had nothing to do with disease. In addition, all that foolish talk about Luke being Paul's physician is not true. Physicians were sorcerers. They belonged to the spiritualistic group. The Greek word *pharmacia*, from which we get the word *pharmacist*, is the word for "sorcerer."

In 2 Corinthians 4:10–11 (ASV), Paul says, *"Always [bear] about in the body the dying of Jesus, that the life also of Jesus may be manifested in our body. For we who live are always delivered unto death for Jesus' sake."*

Why bear *"in the body the dying of Jesus"*? The Corinthians lived in constant fear of being stoned, thrown to the lions, or burned at the stake.

"That the life also of Jesus may be manifested in our body" is a startling statement. God's life reigns in our physical bodies.

Jehovah is the strength of my life; of whom shall I be afraid?
(Psalm 27:1)

Our mortal bodies, our death-doomed bodies, now have the strength of God, the life of God, because Jesus' life is imparted to our physical bodies. That is not healing. That is preservation from sickness. That is protection. That is the strength and power and ability of God in our physical bodies.

So don't try to get your healing. God has given it to you. Don't try to believe. You are a believer, and all things are yours. Don't talk doubt. It only breeds more doubt.

34

FROM THE TOP OF YOUR HEAD TO THE SOLES OF YOUR FEET

DON GOSSETT

Make the following statements a personal confession of faith. These exciting truths will minister complete liberation.

1. I have made an amazing discovery: *"Christ hath redeemed us from the curse of the law, being made a curse for us"* (Galatians 3:13). What was that curse? It is recorded in Deuteronomy 28:15–68—many diseases came upon the people because of disobedience to God's law. It included being afflicted *"from the sole of thy foot unto the top of thy head"* (verse 35).

2. Christ reversed the curse! Christ Jesus has redeemed me from the curse of the law, having been made a curse for me, and thus has reversed the curse and provided healing for me from the top of my head to the soles of my feet! Some folks say, "I can believe the Lord for healing of arthritis and heart trouble but not for cancer." But it's no harder to believe for one disease than it is for

another, for the Lord *"healeth all* [my] *diseases"* (Psalm 103:3).

3. In order for Christ to redeem me from this terrible curse of the law, He was made a curse for me; that is, He bore the punishment prescribed by the law for me. This is why He took *"our infirmities, and bare our sicknesses"* (Matthew 8:17). What a thrill to know that God so loved me that He paid a great price for my redemption—that is, He's redeemed me from Satan! The price of this redemption was the shed blood of His only Son. *"God so loved the world, that he gave his only begotten Son"* (John 3:16).

4. I confess my freedom instead of bondage. I confess that by His stripes, I am healed. I confess my redemption from all diseases. I confess that my redemption from sin and sickness was complete in Jesus! I confess that Satan's dominion over me ended at Calvary, where God freed me from the curse!

5. *"Stand fast therefore in the liberty wherewith Christ hath made us free"* (Galatians 5:1). I am free! I confess that! I tell the devil that I have found out the truth. He's known it all the time, but he has lied to me and blinded my eyes to it. He's kept me from knowing my rights in Christ, my wonderful Redeemer. *"The god of this world hath blinded the minds of them which believe not"* (2 Corinthians 4:4). I tell Satan that I have found out the truth and that the truth has set me free from him! (See John 8:32.)

6. The diseases of my body were laid on Jesus. I never need bear them, because He has borne them. All I need to do is believe this and begin to confess it. I refuse to allow sickness to dwell in my body because I was healed with Jesus' stripes. This is the end of so-called chronic ailments in my body. I will always remember that Satan is a deceiver; he is a liar. Sickness, disease, sin, and

infirmities were all laid on Christ. He bore them. He carried them away and left me free and well. I rejoice in this liberty of mine.

7. I am *"bought with a price: therefore, [I] glorify God in [my] body, and in [my] spirit, which are God's"* (1 Corinthians 6:20).

8. I am delivered. I am loosed. By His stripes, I am healed from the top of my head to the soles of my feet! Thank You, Jesus, for my deliverance!

35

THE ORIGIN OF SICKNESS

E. W. KENYON

It is hard for us to understand that the natural laws that are governing the earth very largely came into being with the fall of man, when the curse came upon the earth. It is because of this that many accuse God of the accidents that take place, of the sickness and death of loved ones, of storms and catastrophes, and of earthquakes and floods that continually occur.

All these natural laws, as we understand them, were set aside by Jesus whenever it was necessary to bless humanity. They came with the fall. Their author is Satan, and when Satan is finally eliminated from human contact, or rather, from the earth, these laws will stop functioning.

Jesus' description of the Father and His declaration that *"he that hath seen me hath seen the Father"* (John 14:9) makes it impossible for us to accept the teaching that disease and sickness are of God.

The Father's very nature refutes the argument that He would use sickness to discipline us or to deepen our piety. In speaking of the woman with the infirmity in Luke 13:16 (ASV),

Jesus plainly taught us that disease is of the adversary:

And ought not this woman, being a daughter of Abraham, whom Satan had bound, lo, these eighteen years, to have been loosed from this bond on the day of the sabbath?

If you will read carefully the four Gospels, you will notice that Jesus was continually casting demons out of sick people, breaking Satan's dominion over the lives of men and women.

In Acts 10:38 (ASV), Peter tells us,

Jesus of Nazareth, how God anointed him with the Holy Spirit and with power: who went about doing good, and healing all that were oppressed of the devil; for God was with him.

In the Great Commission, Jesus said,

These signs shall accompany them that believe: in my name shall they cast out demons; they shall speak with new tongues; they shall take up serpents, and if they drink any deadly thing, it shall in no wise hurt them; they shall lay hands on the sick, and they shall recover.   (Mark 16:17–18 ASV)

There is no such thing as the separation of disease and sickness from Satan. Disease came with the fall of man. You cannot conceive of sickness in the garden of Eden before Adam sinned. The fall was of the adversary. Sickness and sin have the same origin.

Jesus' attitude toward sickness was an uncompromising warfare with Satan. He healed all who were sick. No one ever came to Him who did not receive immediate deliverance.

Jesus' attitude toward sin and His attitude toward sickness were identical. He dealt with sickness as He dealt with demons.

We have been driven to the conclusion that if disease and sickness are of the devil, and we have found that they are, then there is only one attitude that the believer can take toward them: we must follow in Jesus' footsteps and deal with disease as Jesus dealt with it.

HOW GOD DEALT WITH DISEASE UNDER THE FIRST COVENANT

When Israel came out of Egypt, she was God's own covenant people. As soon as that nation had crossed the Red Sea and started toward its homeland, the Angel of the Covenant said to Moses:

> *If thou wilt diligently hearken to the voice of Jehovah thy God, and wilt do that which is right in his eyes, and wilt give ear to his commandments, and keep all his statutes, I will [permit] none of the diseases upon thee, which I have [permitted] upon the Egyptians: for I am Jehovah that healeth thee.*
>
> (Exodus 15:26 ASV)

The student of Hebrew will recognize that I have taken liberty to translate literally the expression "*I will put none of these diseases upon thee.*" I believe it to be a correct translation. God did not put the diseases upon Israel. Neither did He put the diseases upon the Egyptians. It was Satan, the god of this world, who made men sick.

Here Jehovah declares that He is to be Israel's Healer:

> *And ye shall serve Jehovah your God, and he will bless thy bread, and thy water; and I will take sickness away from the midst of thee. There shall none cast her young, nor be barren, in thy land: the number of thy days I will fulfil.*
>
> (Exodus 23:25–26 ASV)

He says He will take sickness from the midst of them. It is a remarkable fact that as long as Israel walked in the covenant, there was no sickness among them.

There is no record of any babies or young people ever having died as long as they kept the covenant.

"*There shall none cast her young.*" There were no miscarriages or abnormal abortions.

There were no barren wives in the land. Every home had children.

"*The number of thy days I will fulfil.*" There were no premature deaths. Every person grew to full age before he laid down his work.

This is remarkable. Jehovah took over that nation. He became their Healer, Protector, and Supplier of every need. He was everything they needed.

> *And he will love thee, and bless thee, and multiply thee; he will also bless the fruit of thy body and the fruit of thy ground, thy grain and thy new wine and thine oil, the increase of thy cattle and the young of thy flock, in the land which he sware unto thy fathers to give thee. Thou shalt be blessed above all peoples: there shall not be male or female barren among you, or among your cattle. And Jehovah will take away from thee all sickness.*   (Deuteronomy 7:13–15 ASV)

Jehovah was to meet every need, supply every demand of that nation. He was to be intimately in contact with every member of the family.

Everything connected with them was to bear the stamp of prosperity and success. Disease and sickness were not to be tolerated among them.

> *And, behold, the acts of Asa, first and last, lo, they are written in the book of the kings of Judah and Israel. And in the thirty and ninth year of his reign Asa was diseased in his feet; his disease was exceeding great: yet in his disease he sought not to Jehovah, but to the physicians. And Asa slept with his fathers.*   (2 Chronicles 16:11–13 ASV)

One can see clearly here that Jehovah was displeased with Asa for seeking the help of man when He had promised to be his Healer.

Carefully read the Psalms, and you will find that God was Israel's Healer. It is continually mentioned.

Who forgiveth all thine iniquities; who healeth all thy diseases; who redeemeth thy life from destruction; who crowneth thee with lovingkindness and tender mercies; who satisfieth thy desire with good things, so that thy youth is renewed like the eagle.   (Psalm 103:3–5 ASV)

The fact that disease came through disobedience to the Law is evident. Forgiveness for disobedience meant the healing of their bodies.

We share with Christ in His resurrection life. We reign as kings in the realm of this resurrection life.

You are what He says you are, whether you recognize it or not. You share in all He is and has done. As He was on earth, you are today. As He is seated at the Father's right hand, legally you are there, too.

36

THE TONGUE OF THE WISE IS HEALTH

DON GOSSETT

Speak the following confessions of health over your life.

1. Jesus promised, *"He shall have whatsoever he saith"* (Mark 11:23). My tongue determines whether I shall have health or sickness, whichever I practice saying.

2. How does my tongue minister health benefits to me? I discipline my tongue to say what God says about my healing and health problems. *"He sent his word, and healed them"* (Psalm 107:20). His Word is my healing portion.

3. My tongue administers health to me when I use it to say, "By His stripes, I am healed." (See Isaiah 53:5; 1 Peter 2:24.) My tongue is the instrument of health when I affirm that Jesus *"Himself took [my] infirmities, and bare [my] sicknesses"* (Matthew 8:17).

4. *"Pleasant words are as an honeycomb, sweet to the soul, and health to the bones"* (Proverbs 16:24). Pleasant

words—that is, words pleasing to God—minister health to me. What are pleasant words? Words that are spoken in harmony with God's wonderful Word.

5. *"Death and life are in the power of the tongue"* (Proverbs 18:21). My tongue has the power to produce death. How? By speaking words of sickness and disease rather than the healing Scriptures. *"Thou art snared with the words of thy mouth, thou art taken with* [captive by] *the words of thy mouth"* (Proverbs 6:2). If I talk about illness and infirmities rather than the healing Word, my *"lips are the snare of* [my] *soul"* (Proverbs 18:7).

6. *"A wholesome tongue is a tree of life"* (Proverbs 15:4). I know that one day, *"the tree of life* [shall be]...*for the healing of the nations"* (Revelation 22:2). My tongue now is a health-producer, for I affirm, "The Lord heals me of all my diseases." (See Psalm 103:3.)

7. *"The tongue of the wise useth knowledge aright"* (Proverbs 15:2). I have full knowledge of the healing Scriptures. My tongue shall affirm them. I say, "I am recovering." (See Mark 16:18.)

8. Jesus Christ is my wisdom and makes me a wise person. (See 1 Corinthians 1:30.) My tongue ministers health to me. God's healing words *"are...health to all* [my] *flesh"* (Proverbs 4:22).

Now thank the Lord for His healing:

I thank You, Jesus, that by Your stripes I am healed. I thank You, Lord, that You took my infirmities and bore my diseases. I bless You, Lord, that You heal all my diseases. I praise You, Lord, that You sent Your Word and healed me. That Word is health to all my flesh right now.

37

THE DISEASE PROBLEM

E. W. KENYON

This is Jesus' spiritual ministry, which began on the cross.

> He was despised, and rejected of men; a man of sorrows, and acquainted with grief: and as one from whom men hide their face he was despised; and we esteemed him not. Surely he hath borne our griefs, and carried our sorrows; yet we did esteem him stricken, smitten of God, and afflicted. But he was wounded for our transgressions, he was bruised for our iniquities; the chastisement of our peace was upon him; and with his stripes we are healed. (Isaiah 53:3–5 ASV)

The disciples could not see it when they looked upon the thorn-crowned Man of Galilee, but He was then bearing our sicknesses and diseases.

Verse 10 (ASV) reads, "Yet it pleased Jehovah to bruise him; he hath put him to grief ["made him sick" (Young's Literal Translation)]." He made Him sin with our sins, sick with our sicknesses.

Isaiah 52:14 (ASV) reads, "His visage was so marred more than any man." It was so marred that He no longer looked like a man.

This was not His physical body; God could not look on His soul *"when [He made] his soul an offering for sin"* (Isaiah 53:10 asv). He was stricken, smitten of God, and afflicted.

It was God who laid our diseases on Him. Jesus was smitten by Justice, because He was our Substitute. *"He was bruised for our iniquities; the chastisement of our peace was upon him; and with his stripes we are healed."*

These were not the physical stripes upon His back made by the Roman lictor but the stripes that God put upon Him with our diseases when He was judged and cast out in our stead.

Matthew 8:17 (asv) says, *"That it might be fulfilled which was spoken through Isaiah the prophet, saying: Himself took our infirmities, and bare our diseases."*

Our infirmities are our little mental quirks, the things that make us disagreeable and unpleasant to people. These are largely infirmities of the mind.

He bore them all. What He bore, we do not need to bear. What He took upon Himself, we need not suffer.

We have come to believe that it is just as wrong for a believer to bear his sickness when Jesus bore it as it is for him to bear his sins when Christ bore them. We have no right to live in sin and to bear those hateful habits that make life a curse, because Christ bore them.

It was wrong for Him to bear them if we are going to bear them, too. It is wrong for us to have sickness and disease in our bodies when God laid those diseases on Jesus. He became sick with our diseases, that we might be healed. He knew no sickness until He was made sick with our diseases. The object of His sin-bearing was to make righteous the ones who believe on Him. The object of disease-bearing was to make well the ones who believe in Him as the disease-bearer.

His sin-bearing made righteousness sure to the new creation. His disease-bearing makes healing sure to the new creation. He took our sins and made us righteous. He took our diseases and made us well. He took our infirmities and gave us His strength. He exchanged His strength for our weakness, His success for our failings.

DISEASE IS NOT THE WILL OF THE FATHER

We understand that disease is broken ease, broken fellowship with heaven. Disease is pain, weakness, and loss of ability to bless and help. It makes slaves of the people who care for the sick. The loved ones who are up night and day working over the sick ones are robbed of joy and rest.

Sickness is not of love, and God is love. Disease is a robber. It steals health. It steals happiness. It steals money we need for other things. Disease is an enemy.

Look at what it steals from a tuberculosis patient. It comes upon him in the midst of young manhood and makes him a burden to his family. It fills him with anxiety and doubt, fear and pain. It robs him of his faith.

See what disease does to a woman who is a wife and mother. It robs her of her beauty and her joy and love. She is no longer able to fill the place of a mother or wife. All this is of the devil.

Jesus said that disease was of Satan:

> *And behold, a woman that had a spirit of infirmity eighteen years; and she was bowed together, and could in no wise lift herself up....And ought not this woman, being a daughter of Abraham, whom Satan had bound, lo, these eighteen years, to have been loosed from this bond...?*   (Luke 13:11, 16 ASV)

She was Satan-bound.

Acts 10:38 (ASV) tells us that Jesus "*went about doing good, and healing all that were oppressed of the devil.*" From the beginning to the end of Jesus' public ministry, He was combated by Satan. His battle was not with men but entirely with demons who indwelt men. It was the devil who used the high priesthood to stir up the strife that finally nailed Jesus to the cross.

Don't let anyone tell you that disease is the will of Love. It is the will of hate—it is the will of Satan. If disease becomes the will of love, love has turned to hatred. If disease is the will of God, heaven will be filled with disease and sickness.

Jesus was the express will of the Father; He went about healing the sick. Disease and sickness are never the will of the Father. To believe that they are is to be disillusioned by the adversary. If healing had not been in the plan of redemption, it would not have been in the substitutionary chapter of Isaiah 53. If healing had not been in redemption, the Father would not have taught it in His Word.

Jesus healed all who came to Him, Jews and Gentiles alike. He was carrying out the will of the Father. He was the will of the Father.

38

A VISION OF THE STRIPING

DON GOSSETT

It has been my privilege to minister the gospel in various cities of New Zealand. From that land, I have received a most remarkable testimony of the striping of Jesus. The account I now share was reported by Henry Gallers of Whanganui, New Zealand.

"Some believers were having a tarrying meeting in Whanganui, and the emphasis that evening concerned the infilling of the Holy Spirit. A young lad of fifteen had been filled with the Spirit, and joy filled the congregation. As his mother looked at her son, however, she was disturbed. He seemed anything by joyful. His face looked pained and drawn and white. She wondered at his unusual appearance.

"Later, that boy explained to us what had been happening to him. As he had been thinking of the great sacrifice Jesus had made for him, he'd had a vision of the scourging of Jesus. That's why he wasn't so joyful. He'd seen our Lord tied up, hanging by the wrists, suspended so that His feet just touched the ground. He'd seen the Roman soldier inflict on Jesus the first blow of his whip. That young man, like many other people, must have thought that because Jesus was meek, he must have been a rather frail-looking, slightly built man. But not at all! The miles that Jesus traveled over those hot, dusty Galilean hills demanded a strong and able body. Also, people forget that Jesus was only thirty-three when He was crucified. In this vision, the lad had seen Jesus' young back and his massive, muscular shoulders—muscular enough to enable Him to carry that heavy cross. No matter how strong His body, however, that cat-o'-nine-tails had cut Him and pained Him just as it would either you or me. The Roman soldier's lash had cut a deep furrow across Jesus' back that day, it had chopped His flesh and scattered blood; but He'd been able to bear it.

"The boy's knowledge of the scourging of Jesus had been very limited prior to this vision. When he'd knelt to pray, he hadn't really had any idea of what a scourging was like. Unexpectedly, though, right before he closed his eyes, he'd had a symbolic vision of what had happened on the spiritual level those centuries ago.

"In his mind's eye, he saw a great mob of people standing around. It was not the mob that had actually witnessed the flogging in Jerusalem but rather a great crowd of cripples and ailing people. Some had had crutches; others different means of support. He'd seen only one of the thirty-nine blows our Lord had received, but as the whip recoiled from that cutting blow, pieces of flesh and drops of blood had flown out over the mob. Miracle of miracles, and with all glory to God, when the tiniest particle of flesh or drop of blood had landed on a person, he was instantly healed; he was made perfectly whole!

"The people were dropping their crutches and walking about, demonstrating their healing. The smallest imaginable droplet of blood from that blow was charged with the power to heal. When you know that Jesus bore not one but thirty-nine stripes, and you know the suffering that He endured, you can realize the healing power that will yet flow for all who will only truly say, 'With His stripes, I am healed.'

"The lad's vision was symbolic. The crowd he'd seen wasn't the crowd that actually witnessed Jesus' flogging. No, we were among the ill and crippled healed by His stripes.

"When the lad rose to his feet, joy flooded his face. He no longer dwelt on the blood and the open wounds of Jesus. He dwelt on the love that Jesus has for us, for in pouring out His blood, He made healing available to all of us."

I cannot overemphasize the quotation "By His stripes, I am healed." I know two things about this phrase: First, the Bible says, *"With his stripes we are healed"* (Isaiah 53:5), *"By whose stripes ye were healed"* (1 Peter 2:24), and *"Himself took our infirmities, and bare our sicknesses"* (Matthew 8:17). Second, you must say what the Bible says to get what the Bible promises. You must put your faith into words. You must develop the habit of quoting God's Word.

When this happens, you will walk in healing.

39

DESTROYING THE WORKS OF THE DEVIL

E. W. KENYON

One of the strongest Scriptures on healing is Romans 8:11 (ASV):

> But if the Spirit of him that raised up Jesus from the dead dwelleth in you, he that raised up Christ Jesus from the dead shall give life also to your mortal bodies through his Spirit that dwelleth in you.

This is physical healing. This is the Holy Spirit taking the life of God and making it efficacious in our physical bodies, making it health and strength and life to us.

This same Holy Spirit who raised the dead body of Jesus is now working in our death-doomed bodies, making them perfect—sickless and sinless.

> He that doeth sin is of the devil; for the devil sinneth from the beginning. To this end was the Son of God manifested, that he might destroy the works of the devil.   (1 John 3:8 ASV)

Jesus did His part of destroying the works of the devil. After He left the earth, He gave us the Holy Spirit, the New Testament, and the ability to use His own name that we, His representatives here on the earth, might go on destroying the works of the devil.

Sin, sickness, and disease in the church today are there because of our not taking our places in Christ. They are there because we have never been trained to do the work that Jesus said we were to do.

Do you think that Jesus would have given us John 14:12 (ASV) if we were not to use it?

> *Verily, verily, I say unto you, he that believeth on me, the works that I do shall he do also; and greater works than these shall he do; because I go unto the Father.*

He meant that we should do greater works than He did, because there are a greater number of us. Our work should be that of destroying the works of the adversary. The weapon we are to use is found in verses 13–14 (ASV):

> *And whatsoever ye shall ask in my name, that will I do, that the Father may be glorified in the Son. If ye shall ask anything in my name, that will I do.*

That word *"ask"* means to demand.

His name is to be used in the sense the way we see it used by Peter who spoke to the impotent man at the gate of the temple, saying, *"In the name of Jesus Christ of Nazareth, walk"* (Acts 3:6 ASV).

This is not prayer. This is casting out demons in Jesus' name. There is healing for the sick in His name. There is power to break disease and sickness in the hearts and lives of men in His name.

Can the name of Jesus keep us from sickness? Can it keep us from want? Can it keep us from poverty, fear, and dread of hunger and cold? Can His name be used just as He suggested in Mark 16:17–18 (ASV)?

> *And these signs shall accompany them that believe: in my name shall they cast out demons; they shall speak with new tongues; they shall take up serpents, and if they drink any deadly thing, it shall in no wise hurt them; they shall lay hands on the sick, and they shall recover.*

The early church was utterly independent of circumstances. I don't mean the whole church. I mean the apostles who fully understood the power of the name of Jesus.

In their day, men were sick because they had broken fellowship with God and lacked knowledge, just as they do today.

The Gentiles in the early church had never had a revelation from God. It was utterly raw material. And the Jews were in even worse condition. They were covenant breakers, just as the modern church is.

The most difficult people to deal with today are the most religious. If there was sickness in the early church, it was to be expected, because they had no precedent, no examples ahead of them.

Jesus came to destroy the works of the devil, and we are His instruments to do His work. We are to destroy sickness in the church. Our new slogan should be, "No more sickness in the body of Christ." His Word is to become a reality in the lives of men.

The fact that He bore our sins and put sin away by sacrificing Himself, and that He provided the remission of all sin, all we have ever done or said, proves that we should not be sick or in bondage to sin.

He made the sacrifice for sins, the things we have done as a result of the sin nature. However, the new birth wipes out everything we have ever done.

Wherefore if any man is in Christ, he is a new creature: the old things are passed away; behold, they are become new.

(2 Corinthians 5:17 ASV)

Furthermore, Romans 8:1 becomes a reality: "*There is therefore now no condemnation to them that are in Christ Jesus.*" The people who are in Christ Jesus are sin free, disease free, and condemnation free.

Let us, arise, then, take our place, and go out and carry this message of deliverance and victory to others.

It is very important that we clearly grasp 1 John 5:13 (ASV):

These things have I written unto you, that ye may know that ye have eternal life, even unto you that believe on the name of the Son of God.

We have God's nature, which gives us a perfect fellowship with the Father, a perfect right to use His name, and a perfect deliverance and freedom from Satan's dominion.

Whereby he hath granted unto us his precious and exceeding great promises; that through these ye may become partakers of the divine nature.   (2 Peter 1:4 ASV)

If ye shall ask anything in my name, that will I do.

(John 14:14 ASV)

For sin shall not have dominion over you.

(Romans 6:14 ASV)

If sin cannot lord itself over you, then disease cannot lord itself over you, because they come from the same source. The nature and life of God that has come into you will give you life and health.

With long life will I satisfy him, and show him my salvation.

(Psalm 91:16 ASV)

We all admit that Psalm 91 belongs to the church. It may have not applied to the Jew, but it does apply to us.

He will cover thee with his pinions, and under his wings shalt thou take refuge: his truth [or Word] is a shield and a buckler. Thou shalt not be afraid for the terror by night, nor for the arrow that flieth by day; for the pestilence that walketh in darkness, nor for the destruction that wasteth at noonday. A thousand shall fall at thy side, and ten thousand at thy right hand; but it shall not come nigh thee.   (Psalm 91:4–7 ASV)

There is protection from earthquakes, cyclones, pestilence, sickness, and war. This puts us into the realm of the supernatural. We are linked with Christ, for He said, "*I am the vine, ye are the branches*" (John 15:5 ASV). The life in the Vine is in the branch. As soon as the branch is wounded, the Vine pours life into it, so that it can go on bearing fruit. So the life of God pours into the body of Christ and heals the members of sickness, disease, and want, so that they can go on bearing fruit to the glory of God.

Worry and fear poison the blood stream; faith in the Lord Jesus purifies it. Disease gains ascendency when you confess the testimony of your senses, but it is defeated when you confess the Word. Satan is whipped with words; you are healed with words.

Make your lips do their duty. Fill them with His Word.

40

TRAIN WRECK VICTIM

DON GOSSETT

While I was engaged in a large tent meeting in Fresno, California, I met a minister named Jack Neville. His testimony was a real blessing to my life, so I will share it with you.

Jack had been involved in a serious track wreck in Fresno. Along with other accident victims, he had been rushed to the hospital and was in serious condition. The doctors took X-rays and, upon discovering that he was a minister, they felt that they could level with him about the severity of his injuries.

"Reverend," they said, "we want you to know what the X-rays have revealed. Your back is badly broken. In your present condition, we're not certain that you'll make it. If you do live, you'll probably never walk again."

Jack had been experienced in coping with the unexpected, but this was simply too much! He felt inwardly crushed.

As he rehearsed those words over and over in his mind, he found himself crying, "Oh, God, the doctors have told me that I may not live. And, Lord, they said that even if I do live, I'll probably never walk again. Lord, I'd rather You take me home today. My life is Yours to preach the gospel. But, Lord, with the knowledge that I won't be able to stand in the pulpit any longer, I'd prefer to die today."

As he continued to plead with God to take his life, suddenly the words from Matthew 8:17 flashed across his mind: *"Himself took our infirmities, and bare our sicknesses."*

As he meditated on this truth, the reality of it broke through to his heart. The Holy Spirit revealed to him that Jesus had actually taken his injuries upon Himself when He was scourged for our healing. Jesus Himself took our infirmities and bore our sicknesses, our diseases, and our afflictions.

As the wonder of this great truth gripped his heart, fresh hope sprang up. Suddenly, Jack was transformed from a self-pitying Christian into a rejoicing believer who had discovered what a great Redeemer he had and what a mighty redemption had been provided by the Lord.

The significance of the bleeding wounds of Jesus held his attention. The truth *"with his stripes we are healed"* (Isaiah 53:5) was no longer a worn-out phrase to him. Each word throbbed with life and healing for Jack's broken body. He began to praise the Lord with his whole heart.

He would say, "Dear Jesus, if You took my infirmities and carried my sickness in Your own body, then I don't need to bear them. Lord, it just isn't necessary that I endure this broken and crushed body, when You have already taken this suffering upon Yourself. Thank You, Jesus, that by Your stripes, I am healed!"

After some time, Jack made his decision: There was no need for him to remain in the hospital with that hopeless verdict upon his life. According to the provisions of Jesus, he had already been healed! Why should he remain captive to that bed?

Finally, he exercised his faith and decided to get up out of the bed. With praises to Jesus flowing from his heart and mouth, he stepped down on the floor and found that he was amazingly strong!

Quickly, he dressed and walked out of the hospital room. In the hall, he met his attending nurse. She looked at him as if she had seen a ghost. "Reverend Neville," she sputtered, "you...can't!"

"Can't what, nurse?" he replied calmly.

Her reply was fervent: "Your legs, your back, Reverend—they're broken! It's impossible! Get back to your room before you fall over dead!"

"Thank you, nurse," he responded politely, "but I'm walking out of this place. You see, Jesus, my Great Physician, has paid me a visit and made me whole."

With those parting words, Jack proceeded down the hallway to the checkout desk. Before he could complete his checkout, however, the nurse had summoned his attending physicians. They rushed over to the desk, approached him with caution, then appealed to him. "Reverend, we don't know what happened, or how you walked down here, but we do know your condition—you just can't do this."

They had already called for a stretcher. When it arrived, they tried rather desperately to get him to lie down on it. Once again, though, he shared his testimony: "Jesus, the Great Physician, paid me a visit and has made me whole."

Seeing Jack standing there straight and strong, then bending over to demonstrate how well he was, they couldn't deny it.

Later, he returned to the hospital for X-rays and a thorough examination. The doctors acknowledged that they could find nothing wrong with him. They agreed that mysteriously, the Great Physician had done His work.

I had the occasion to interview Jack Neville at length. He had personally written his own book about God's wonderful miracle for him. It contained testimonials of verification written by doctors and other health professionals involved in his case.

Jack emphasized how important the revelation of the bleeding stripes of Jesus was for his miraculous healing! The combination of speaking "By His stripes, I am healed" and praising the Lord brought an awesome miracle for a hopeless pastor!

Remember, Jesus took your infirmities and bore your diseases. By His stripes, you, too, are healed. Confess it and possess it. To God be the glory!

41

THE ABUNDANT LIFE

E. W. KENYON

Christianity is a living reality. Jesus said, *"I came that they may have life, and may have it abundantly"* (John 10:10 ASV). It is the abundance of life that gives healing, strength, and energy.

"Casting all your anxiety upon him, because he careth for you" (1 Peter 5:7 ASV). This means that in the mind of the Father, there has come an end to worry, fear, and doubt. The work of the adversary has been destroyed.

The following promise was given to the Jews under the first covenant, but it may become a living, sweet reality to us, too:

> *And ye shall serve Jehovah your God, and he will bless thy bread, and thy water; and I will take sickness away from the midst of thee. There shall none cast her young, nor be barren, in thy land: the number of thy days I will fulfil.*
> (Exodus 23:25–26 ASV)

Is our covenant as good as that?

And my God shall supply every need of yours according to his riches [unveiled] in Christ Jesus."   (Philippians 4:19 ASV)

I can do all things in him that strengtheneth me.
(Philippians 4:13)

Not that I speak in respect of want: for I have learned, in whatsoever state I am, therein to be content.
(Philippians 4:11 ASV)

We rise into the realm of the supernatural as absolute overcomers, perfect victors in Christ. Is it any wonder that Paul, at the close of the Romans 8, declares, *"Nay, in all these things we are more than conquerors"* (Romans 8:37 ASV)?

There is nothing that can separate us from the love of God as unveiled in Christ Jesus, our Lord.

He that spared not his own Son, but delivered him up for us all, how shall he not also with him freely give us all things?
(Romans 8:32 ASV)

We stand upon the mount of victory. Now we can say, "There is no more sickness in the body of Christ."

His Word is a reality in the lives of the sons of God. We are going out today to destroy the works of the enemy in the bodies, minds, and spirits of men.

There are several methods of healing, but the one that stands first in the mind of the Spirit is found in Isaiah 53:4–6 (ASV):

Surely he hath borne our griefs, and carried our sorrows; yet we did esteem him stricken, smitten of God, and afflicted. But he was wounded for our transgressions, he was bruised for our iniquities; the chastisement of our peace was upon him; and with his stripes we are healed. All we like sheep have gone astray; we have turned every one to his own way; and Jehovah hath laid on him the iniquity of us all.

He was stricken and smitten with our diseases. Sin and sickness are one in the mind of the Father. God is against anything that touches and injures man. Disease touches the man, and God lays it upon Jesus. Sin touches a man, and God lays it upon Jesus.

When He declares that by His stripes we are healed, that means that we are freed from sickness. That is our receipt in full for a sickless and sinless life, for sin and disease shall not have dominion over us. (See Romans 6:14.)

Furthermore, we know that the blood of Jesus Christ cleanses us from sin.

But if we walk in the light, as he is in the light, we have fellowship one with another, and the blood of Jesus his Son cleanseth us from all sin. (1 John 1:7 ASV)

If we have committed sin, we have an Advocate with the Father.

My little children, these things write I unto you that ye may not sin. And if any man sin, we have an Advocate with the Father, Jesus Christ the righteous. (1 John 2:1 ASV)

We must take what belongs to us as sons and daughters of God.

We know that if we confess our sins, He will forgive us and cleanse us.

If we confess our sins, he is faithful and righteous to forgive us our sins, and to cleanse us from all unrighteousness.
(1 John 1:9 ASV)

We come to Him with all our diseases, knowing that they all were laid on Jesus. Knowing this, it is not right that we should bear them. The adversary has no right to put diseases on us, because they were laid on Christ.

I can say to the Father, "Do you see what the adversary has done in my body? In the name of Jesus, I take deliverance from this thing Satan has afflicted me with."

I whisper to my heart, "By His stripes, I am healed." Then the pain must go. Multitudes are being healed like that today through our ministry. We can be just as free from diseases as we are free from bad habits; after all, the habit of sickness is just like any other unclean habit.

There is provision made for a perfect healing. None of us need suffer in the hand of the enemy. Your deliverance is in the redemptive work of Christ.

42

WORDS OF LIFE: "BY HIS STRIPES, I AM HEALED"

DON GOSSETT

I want to share one of the most heart-warming stories I've ever encountered on my travels in fifty-six nations. It happened when I was in Parsons, Kansas, and Pastor Lewis Greenfeather, a Native American, invited me to minister at his church on Sunday and Monday.

On Monday, he described to me a man named Bruce who had recently received Christ as his Savior and Lord. However, Bruce had suffered a paralytic stroke, and Pastor Greenfeather asked if I would accompany him to Bruce's home to pray for his healing. So, before I left Parsons, we went to his home.

There, I witnessed the usual consequences of a stroke—Bruce's mouth was disfigured, his left hand was useless, and he was unable to walk even a step. Pastor Greenfeather informed me that Bruce had received no instructions on how to receive his healing, so he asked me to explain them to him.

Gladly, I did so. "Bruce, healing from the Lord is based entirely on what His Word teaches. In some of the Master's final words, He shared a valuable truth. He said, *'These signs shall follow them that believe; in my name…they shall lay hands on the sick, and they shall recover'* (Mark 16:17–18). This does not guarantee that when hands are laid on you, you shall recover instantly. Our part is to obey the Lord and lay hands on you. Jesus' part is to enable you to recover your health."

It looked as if Bruce, with all simplicity, understood this assurance. I explained to him about the bleeding stripes Jesus took upon Himself for our healing. Then I read Isaiah 53:5: *"With his stripes we are healed."*

"Bruce," I stated, "A big Roman soldier lashed Jesus' body thirty-nine times, that we might have healing. In that vicious striping, Jesus bore all our sickness, disease, pain, and affliction in His body. Because He did this for us in love, healing is ours. As God sees us, we are already healed because of what Jesus suffered for us. It cost the Son of God so very much. Willingly, He became our Substitute, that we might be healed.

"I have noticed here in your home that you have a big clock that chimes every hour. Bruce, when you hear the next chime, signifying that another hour has passed, let that be the time you speak out, 'Thank You, Jesus, that by Your stripes, I am healed.'"

It was not easy for Bruce to speak words because of the paralyzation of his face and mouth, but with all the effort he could muster up, he assured me he would say, "Thank You, Jesus, that by Your stripes, I am healed."

I left Parsons, Kansas, that Monday night. On the following Thursday, Pastor Greenfeather received a phone call from Bruce. "Come out, Pastor," he exclaimed, "I have something wonderful I want you to see."

Pastor Greenfeather went to Bruce's home. The same man who virtually had been imprisoned to his bed of suffering stood in the living room smiling and declaring, 'It worked just as Don Gossett assured me! I exclaimed in faith, 'Thank You, Jesus, that by Your stripes, I am healed,' and the Lord has healed me!"

Bruce's fingers were straightened out, his legs were normal, and the disfigurement of his face and mouth were all gone. Bruce was completely healed of the dreaded paralytic stroke!

I relate this miraculous story that you may realize the importance of rising up with a new testimony that harmonizes with the Word of God. Hold fast to that affirmation without wavering. God, who has given us His Word, will watch over that Word to perform it! (See Hebrews 4:14; 10:23.)

This is a challenge of utmost importance to you. Begin to speak, "Thank You, Jesus, that by Your stripes, I am healed." Believe it in your heart. See Christ bearing your infirmities and diseases in His own body. Then realize that through those bleeding stripes, He provided healing for you. Now repeat with your whole heart, "Thank You, Jesus, that by Your stripes, I am healed." These are not magic words. They are words that agree with God's Word. God watches over His Word to perform it. (See Jeremiah 1:12.)

I believe it will happen for you.

43

JESUS AND HIS NAME ARE ONE

E. W. KENYON

Jesus and His name are one, just as you and your name are one. You do not have to make this liberty yours. All you have to do is enjoy it and walk in the light of the Word.

Make these facts your confession. If we speak words of faith instead of words of doubt, we will be speaking God's language. Doubt words come from another source. You cannot talk sickness and disease and walk in health. You cannot tell folk about your disease and your pains, and moan over your troubles to get sympathy, without losing your fellowship with Him.

When we tell our troubles to people, we lose our faith and sweet fellowship with the Father. We tell people our troubles to get their sympathy when we should cast our anxiety and troubles upon Him, for He cares for us.

When we talk about our weakness and failure and disease, we glorify the devil, who gave them to us. We glorify doctors and lawyers by taking our troubles to them. They get paid for listening to people's troubles. That is the secret of their success—being good "trouble" listeners.

Speaking our troubles caused by Satan is a confession that Satan is the master and that he has gained the supremacy. It makes the troubles bigger; it makes the disease worse; it makes us feel worse.

Our confessions should be of God's ability and faithfulness, and that our troubles are being borne by Jesus, just as He bore our diseases and sins.

Hold fast to your confession of what God is to you and who you are in Christ.

Give up your confession of Satan's supremacy. You know that disease comes from the adversary, that lack of ability comes from the adversary. All our troubles are demon-made. If you are using demon-inspired words, don't expect to have the sweetest fellowship with heaven.

It is the Word of faith that we speak. Our lips are filled with the Word of faith. Our hearts are singing the song of faith. Jesus said, *"Verily, verily, I say unto you, He that believeth hath eternal life"* (John 6:47 asv).

It is the believer who possesses. I believe, therefore I have. Then I rejoice in my possession and enjoy my possession. Health is my possession. Success is my possession.

I have plenty because God is my Supply. He meets my every need according to His riches in glory in Christ Jesus. (See Philippians 4:19.)

I am not moaning and groaning; I am praising and rejoicing. Faith possesses, and faith's possessions are real, just as real as sense possessions. Spiritual things are as real as material things.

Scripture says, *"For we walk by faith, not by sight"* (2 Corinthians 5:7 asv). We walk in the realm of God. We not only walk by faith, but we talk by faith. We have left the realm of the senses.

When you learn to talk by faith, the dominion of disease will be broken over you. But as long as you walk by reason and follow the suggestions of the senses—feeling, seeing, hearing, and so forth—you will live and walk in the realm of disease, which will hold sway over your life. Pain will hold a carnival in your body.

If you will learn to talk faith talk, you will be a victor. First John 5:4 (ASV) should be known by every believer. It should be a part of your conscious knowledge that you can use day by day.

For whatsoever is begotten of God overcometh the world: and this is the victory that hath overcome the world, even our faith.

44

THE VALUE OF CONFESSION

E. W. KENYON

It is necessary to continually confess our redemption from Satan's dominion and that he no longer rules us with condemnation or fear of disease. We hold fast to this confession, as our confession is Satan's defeat.

We believers do not ask to be healed, because we have been healed. We do not ask to be made righteous, because we have been made righteous. (See 2 Corinthians 5:21.) We do not ask to be redeemed, for our redemption is an absolute fact.

In the mind of the Father, we are perfectly healed and perfectly free from sin, because He laid our diseases and our sins upon His Son. His Son was made sin with our sins and was made sick with our diseases.

In the mind of Christ, we are perfectly healed because He can remember when He was made sin with our sins, when He was made sick with our diseases. He remembers when He put our sin and our diseases away.

In the mind of the Holy Spirit, we are absolutely free from both, for He remembers when Christ was made sin and made sick. He remembers when He raised Jesus from the dead.

Christ was free from our sin and our sickness. Both had been put away before His resurrection. The Word declares, *"With his stripes we are healed"* (Isaiah 53:5). The whole problem is not recognizing the absolute truthfulness of that Word. It is not in good taste to ask God to heal us, for He has already done it.

This truth came with a shock when I first saw it. He declared that we are healed; therefore, we are. The only task now is to get into perfect harmony with His Word. If He declares we are healed, then our part is to thank Him for the work He has already accomplished!

Now I feel I should introduce another subject—the renewing of our minds. It is only the renewed mind that can grasp these truths. Your spirit has been recreated but not your mind. Until now, it has received all its knowledge through the senses, so it must be renewed.

Romans 12:2 (ASV) says, *"And be not fashioned according to this world: but be ye transformed by the renewing of your mind, and ye may prove what is the good and acceptable and perfect will of God."*

The same truth is brought out in the following Scriptures.

Not by works done in righteousness, which we did ourselves, but according to his mercy he saved us, through the washing of regeneration and renewing of the Holy Spirit.

(Titus 3:5 ASV)

And that ye be renewed in the spirit of your mind, and put on the new man, that after God hath been created in righteousness and holiness of truth. (Ephesians 4:23–24 ASV)

And have put on the new man, that is being renewed unto knowledge after the image of him that created him.

(Colossians 3:10 ASV)

This renewing of the mind comes through meditation and action on the Word.

As soon as a person is born again, he should ask the Holy Spirit to come in and make His home in his body. Luke 11:13 shows the Father's attitude in regard to it:

> How much more shall your heavenly Father give the Holy Spirit to them that ask him?

As surely as we ask Him, so surely will the Spirit make His home in our bodies.

The renewed mind sees that all there is to be done for its healing is to praise the Father for it. It says, "My diseases were laid on Christ, and He put them away. I am healed. I thank the Father that it is done."

The pain may be there, the soreness may be there, but these are only the testimony of the senses. We refuse to listen to the witness of our senses. We accept the Word of God and act upon it. As surely as God sits on the throne, He will make that Word good in us.

We do not ask for power, for He who is the Power is in us. We do not ask for wisdom, for Christ was made wisdom unto us. We do not ask for redemption, for He is our redemption. We do not ask for sanctification, for He is made unto us sanctification. We do not ask for righteousness, because He is made unto us righteousness. (See 1 Corinthians 1:30.)

This faith life is the most beautiful thing in the world. We enter it when we step out of the old sense realm where we have lived. Indeed, we have always lived with Thomas, who said, "*Except I shall see in [Christ's] hands the print of the nails, and put my finger into the print of the nails, and thrust my hand into his side, I will not believe*" (John 20:25).

Jesus met him and said, *"Reach hither thy finger, and behold my hands; and reach hither thy hand, and thrust it into my side: and be not faithless, but believing"* (verse 27).

Then Thomas cried, *"My LORD and my God"* (verse 28).

But Jesus said to him, *"Because thou hast seen me, thou hast believed: blessed are they that have not seen, and yet have believed"* (verse 29).

We should not need the evidence of the senses. Let us rest on the Word. Ephesians 1:3 says, *"Blessed be the God and Father of our Lord Jesus Christ, who hath blessed us with all spiritual blessings in the heavenly places in Christ."*

You are in the family. Everything that the Father has belongs to the children. You are one of them. You have been blessed.

45

BY HIS STRIPES, WE ARE HEALED

DON GOSSETT

Have you heard the good news—that by Jesus' stripes, you are healed? The following story will help illustrate this vital truth:

A sea captain named John Cook had been a sailing veteran on the high seas for many years. His personal habits were a dissipated lifestyle. Cook never gave any attention to death or what would happen to him, and he chose an immoral pathway.

On a particular voyage, Captain Cook was stricken deathly ill. The disease had ravaged his body, and the ship doctor told him that he would soon die.

Realizing his desperate physical condition, Cook prayed to God with a sense of urgency. He called for his first mate, whom he pleaded with to pray or read from the Bible to him. Sadly, the first mate told him he didn't know how to pray and couldn't help him find God.

The captain hurriedly found his next officer and gasped, "Please help me find God; I am a dying man."

This man shook his head regretfully; he didn't know how to pray, either. As he left the ship's cabin, his breathing became more labored.

The intensity of the pain only increased, so Captain Cook sent for a lieutenant, with whom he pleaded. He asked him if he would be able to help him find God. Again, he received a dismal reply: "I can't help you, captain. I'm not a praying man."

This response crushed the captain's hope of receiving help from anyone on the ship. But as the third officer left the cabin, he told the captain that he remembered seeing the cook's helper reading a Bible a few days before.

Captain Cook exclaimed, "Send for the boy—quick! Tell him to bring his Bible. Somebody must help me; I'm a dying man!"

The cook's helper was a slender-faced teenage boy named Willie Pratt. Willie had left his home a few months before, when the ship set out on the latest voyage. Nervously and slowly, Willie made his entrance into the captain's presence, thinking he was going to be reprimanded for having a Bible.

John Cook asked Willie to pray for him and to read the Bible to him. Willie told the captain about his mother, who was a Christian woman for as long as Willie could remember. She had always read the Bible to him and prayed for him every night for many years. When Willie left home, it broke his mother's heart. But, knowing his desire to see the world, she helped him pack and appealed to him to read the Bible every day.

Willie confessed to the captain that he had not given his Bible much attention. Recently, however, he had begun to think about his mother's request and about living the right kind of life. He said to the captain, "I'd like to read from a place in the Bible my mother used to read to me."

The captain nodded.

Willie turned to Isaiah 53, verse 5, and read, "*He was wounded for our transgressions, he was bruised for our iniquities: the chastisement of our peace was upon him; and with his stripes we are healed.*"

He looked at the captain and said, "Sir, I'd like to do as my mother taught me, and put my name in there and make it personal for me."

The captain said, "Son, go right ahead."

With tears streaming down his face, his heart softened by the Spirit of God, Willie read the Scripture like this: "He was wounded for Willie's transgressions, He was bruised for Willie's iniquities: the chastisement of Willie's peace was upon Him; and with His stripes, Willie is healed."

The captain was deeply convinced of his own need for Jesus Christ and asked Willie, "Will you read that passage again and put my name in there?"

Solemnly, Willie read Isaiah 53:5 again. "He was wounded for John Cook's transgressions, He was bruised for John Cook's iniquities: the chastisement of John cook's peace was upon Him; and with His stripes, John Cook is healed."

With the reality of what these two men had done, both Willie and John sobbed softly. They knew that their sins had been forgiven, for Jesus had suffered in their place. By making a personal application of God's Word, the captain affirmed, "With His stripes, I, John Cook, am healed." And he was!

It's a remarkable story. Both Willie and John were forgiven their sins, and John was healed. I encourage you to put your name in this verse of God's Word. I believe that you, too, will experience the joy and blessing of sins forgiven and infirmities healed as you realize that Jesus Christ suffered, bled, and died in your place. He came to give His life so that you may go free.

I have led thousands of people in making this Scripture personal, and the results have been wonderful. I've received many testimonies from others who have personalized this verse and received the Lord's benefits.

So speak these words of God:

"With his stripes [I am] *healed"* (Isaiah 53:5).

"By whose stripes [I was] *healed"* (1 Peter 2:24).

"Himself took [my] *infirmities, and bare* [my] *sicknesses"* (Matthew 8:17).

"The same Lord over all is rich unto all that call upon him" (Romans 10:12).

46

THE LIVING WORD

E. W. KENYON

The problem of healing is a problem of the integrity of the Word. Many have never recognized it, but the Word is the healer today. God, in Christ, wrought a perfect redemption. In that redemption is perfect healing for every believer; but, lacking knowledge of the Word, Christians everywhere are sick.

Psalm 107:20 perfectly illustrates this: *"He sent his word, and healed them."* So does John 1:1: *"In the beginning was the Word, and the Word was with God, and the Word was God."* Verse 14 (ASV) reads, *"And the Word became flesh, and dwelt among us (and we beheld his glory, glory as of the only begotten from the Father), full of grace and truth."*

That is the Word He sent. He had sent His spoken Word through the prophets. The living Word was made flesh. Now He unveils the life-giving Word in the Gospels and the Epistles.

The words that I have spoken unto you are spirit, and are life. (John 6:63 ASV)

For the Logos of God is a living thing, active and more cutting than any sword with double edge, penetrating to the very division of soul and spirit, joints and marrow—scrutinizing the very thoughts and conceptions of the heart.

(Hebrews 4:12 MOFFATT)

The Word becomes a living thing only as we act upon it.

The Word is God speaking. It is always a present-tense fact. You might say that the Word is always now, just as God is always now. The Word is also a part of God, Himself. God and His Word are one, just as you and your word are one. And the Word is the will of the Father, just as Jesus, the Word made flesh, was the will of the Father during His earthly ministry.

What God says, is; what God says, will become. Had He not wanted it to be, He would not have said it. Furthermore, you can depend upon His Word utterly. You have depended upon institutions and men. Institutions may fail, individuals may die, nations may disintegrate, but God cannot deny Himself. Behind the Word is the integrity of God. Not only is His integrity behind the Word, but His very throne is involved in His Word. Hebrews 7:22 (ASV) declares that Jesus is the surety of the new covenant: *"By so much also hath Jesus become the surety of a better covenant."* He is behind every word from Matthew to Revelation. Every word was God-breathed. The throne upon which Jesus is seated is behind every Word.

FAITH, HOPE, AND MENTAL ASSENT

There must be a clear distinction in your mind between believing and mental assent. Believing the Word is acting on the Word. Mental assent is acknowledging the truthfulness of the Word, the integrity of the Word, but never acting upon it. Mental assent is standing outside a bakery and coveting the cake in the window but not possessing.

Hope is not faith. It is not believing. Hope is always living in the future. However, faith is always now. It is not passivity, for passivity lies quietly without action, without choice, inert. Faith is acting on the Word. Believing the Word is not only recognizing its utter truthfulness but also taking it to be your very own.

To act on God's Word is to do His will and to act in His will. He is honored by our acting on the Word. He is dishonored by our mentally assenting to its truthfulness, by our hoping that it will become true sometime, and by our passivity that lies quietly rejoicing in the Word but has no part in it. "He that believeth… hath…." (See John 3:36; 6:47.) If you believe, you have!

God's name is glorified by our acting on the Word. The Father is glorified by our acting on the Word. Remember that His throne backs His Word. His integrity is involved in it. Jesus said,

> If ye abide in me, and my words abide in you, ask whatsoever ye will, and it shall be done unto you. Herein is my Father glorified, that ye bear much fruit; and so shall ye be my disciples.
> (John 15:7–8 ASV)

That is the fruit of the indwelling Word, which has prompted answered prayers.

THE CASE STATED

There are two views of healing. The most common view is that healing is not in the redemptive work of Christ but belongs to us if we have faith enough to claim it. This belief holds that faith is the gift of God. If God gives you faith for your healing, you will be healed. If He does not give you faith, there is no need to struggle for your healing. Your only hope is the arm of flesh.

This view is superficial. It is the result of sense knowledge—the knowledge of natural man that is gained through the senses. It is the knowledge taught in all our technical schools and universities.

The other kind of knowledge is revelation knowledge. It teaches that miracles are for today. Sense knowledge repudiates this in a very large measure, because it is above the knowledge of the senses.

The second view of healing is that it is a part of the plan of redemption, that disease came with the fall and is a work of the adversary. Because disease came with the fall, God is the natural, logical healer.

Man cannot deal with the sin problem. He cannot make himself righteous. He cannot rid himself of sin-consciousness. These can only come through the finished work of Christ. God planned that when we were recreated (recreation that comes through our receiving the nature and life of God), we would be righteous and partake of His righteousness, which is His very nature. This would give us the position of sons.

The new creation is more than being baptized or confirmed. It is receiving the life and nature of the Father. Our spirits are recreated by receiving eternal life.

Isaiah 53 holds the key of redemption: Jesus was made sin with our sins. Not only was He made sin with our sins, but He was made sick with our sicknesses.

Natural man is called sin: *"Be not unequally yoked with unbelievers: for what fellowship have righteousness and iniquity? or what communion hath light with darkness?"* (2 Corinthians 6:14 ASV). The believer is called *"righteousness"*; the unbeliever is called *"iniquity."* He has not only committed sin; he is sin. Furthermore, the believer is called *"light,"* and the unbeliever is called *"darkness."* Just as the sinner is "sin," the sick man is not only sick but "sickness." Sin deals with the spirit; sickness is a spiritual thing revealed in the body.

"And what concord hath Christ with Belial?" (2 Corinthians 6:15 ASV). The believer is called *"Christ,"* because Christ is a part of the body. The branch is a part of the Vine. It is as much a part of the Vine as the Vine Himself. (See John 15:5.)

> *For as the body is one, and hath many members, and all the*
> *members of the body, being many, are one body; so also is*
> *Christ.*   (1 Corinthians 12:12 ASV)

The man outside of Christ is called *"Belial."* That perfectly agrees with 1 John 3:10: *"In this the children of God are manifest, and the children of the devil."*

When God laid our sin on Jesus, He laid us on Jesus. He laid the whole man on Jesus. He laid his sins, his weaknesses, his infirmities and diseases, and his union with the adversary on Jesus. Jesus became sin with our sin, became sick with our sickness.

Isaiah 53:10 (ASV) reads, *"Yet it pleased Jehovah to bruise him; he hath put him to grief."* Verse 6 (ASV) reads, *"All we like sheep have gone astray; we have turned every one to his own way; and Jehovah hath laid on him the iniquity of us all."*

AFFLICTED IN SPIRIT

Jesus was made sick with our sicknesses. He was made sin with our sin. This was God's method of dealing with the sin problem. He settled the sin problem, so there is no sin problem. Christ put sin away and satisfied the claims of justice for man. There is no sickness problem; the real problem is the "sinner problem." There is simply a problem of the believer's coming to know his inheritance in Christ.

When John the Baptist said, *"Behold, the Lamb of God, that taketh away the sin of the world!"* (John 1:29 ASV), he was giving public notice that this Man whom he had baptized was the Sin-Substitute, the Sickness-Substitute, for the human race.

Sin and sickness come from the same source—Satan is the author of both. I am sure that it is God's order that the believer should be as free from sickness as he is from sin. He should be as free from the fear of disease as he is from the condemnation of sin.

God cannot see sin in the new creation; neither can He see sickness in the new creation.

James wrote, "Is any sick among you?" (See James 5:14.) There should not be any sick among you, but if there is anyone sick, this tells what he should do. It was the plan of the Father that every believer should know what Peter tells us in 1 Peter 2:24 (ASV): *"Who his own self bare our sins in his body upon the tree, that we, having died unto sins, might live unto righteousness; by whose stripes ye were healed."* He wants us to know that when He laid our sins and sicknesses on Jesus and Jesus bore them away, it was to the end that sin, and disease should no longer have dominion over us. He wants us to know in the second place that sickness and disease do not belong in the family of God.

If there should be any sickness among us, it is because of a low state of knowledge of our rights and privileges in our redemption. It is due to a lack of knowledge of the fact that God, by laying our diseases on Christ, has settled the disease problem in redemption.

At the new birth, sins are all remitted. The sin nature is displaced by the nature of God, and disease leaves with the sins. So the Father can see no sickness in the new creation. He put it all on Christ.

When we recognize the fact that our sickness has been laid on Christ, and that He bore our diseases in His body on the tree, and that by His stripes we are healed, it will be the end of the dominion of disease in our lives.

But this knowledge is of no value until your heart says, "Surely, He bore my diseases and my pains, and by His stripes I am healed," just as though you were the only sick person in the world.

The Word is like God—eternal. It cannot be destroyed. He watches over it to make it good. His Word brought man into being, and now He is building Himself into man through the Word. The Word is part of Himself, and it is this Self that is changing the conduct of believers and bringing them into harmony with Him.

He shares Himself with us; He gives us His nature in the new creation; He makes Himself one with us. We are united with Him in the new birth.

We are to take advantage of this union. His nature gives us new ability and new wisdom, and we must take advantage of it. His strength is ours. His life is ours. His health is ours. His ability is ours.

Disease is Satan's work. When you tell anyone of it, you glorify him. You ignore the fact that God laid that disease upon Jesus and put it away.

The Word says that you are healed. Get used to acting on the Word.

ABOUT THE AUTHORS

E. W. KENYON

Dr. E. W. Kenyon (1867–1948) was born in Saratoga County, New York. At age nineteen, he preached his first sermon. He pastored several churches in New England and founded the Bethel Bible Institute in Spencer, Massachusetts. (The school later became the Providence Bible Institute when it was relocated to Providence, Rhode Island.) Kenyon served as an evangelist for over twenty years. In 1931, he became a pioneer in Christian radio on the Pacific Coast with his show *Kenyon's Church of the Air*, where he earned the moniker "The Faith Builder." He also began the New Covenant Baptist Church in Seattle. In addition to his pastoral and radio ministries, Kenyon wrote extensively.

ABOUT THE AUTHORS

DON GOSSETT

Born again at the age of twelve, **Don Gossett** (1929–2014) served the Lord in active ministry for sixty-six years as pastor, worldwide evangelist, missionary, and longtime broadcaster. He apprenticed with many well-known evangelists, including William Freeman, Raymond T. Richey, Jack Coe, and T. L. Osborn. Don's many writings have been translated into almost twenty languages and have exceeded twenty-five million copies in worldwide distribution. Don raised five children with his first wife, Joyce, who died in 1991. In 1995, Don found lifelong love again and married Debra, an anointed teacher of the Word. They ministered worldwide and lived in British Columbia, Canada, and in Blaine, Washington State.

Don coauthored several books using the writings of E. W. Kenyon, including *The Power of Your Words*, *Keys to Receiving Miracles*, *Speak Life*, *There's a Miracle in Your Mouth*, and *Words that Move Mountains*. For more information about Don Gossett Ministries, go to www.dongossett.com.